"YOU'VE GOT TO BE KID-DING!"
A LOOK AT ADOLESCENTS

"YOU'VE GOT TO BE KID-DING!"
A LOOK AT ADOLESCENTS

Helen Ryley, M.S.

Don Dinkmeyer, Ph.D.
Ed Frierson, Ph.D.
H. Stephen Glenn, Ph.D.
Don Shaw, M.A.

AMERICAN TRAINING CENTER, INC.

THE AUTHOR

Helen Ryley, M.S., author, administrator, educator. She is Vice President of Program Design and Development for American Training Center, Inc. Helen has specialized in adult training, human relations development and the design of multimedia programs. She is included in Who's Who in the West. She has written numerous articles, edited several books, and designed and developed the program *DISCIPLINE WITH LOVE AND LOGIC.*

FEATURE CONSULTANTS

Don Dinkmeyer, Ph.D., national and international consultant, is a Diplomate of the American Board of Professional Psychology. He is the author of twelve books including *The Encouragement Book.* He is also co-author of the parent and teacher training programs, *Systematic Training For Effective Parenting (S.T.E.P.), S.T.E.T. and S.T.E.P. Teen.* These programs have been translated for use in countries throughout the world.

Ed Frierson, Ph.D., lecturer, professor, conference and convention speaker throughout the United States and Canada. He has authored over 50 articles and papers. Dr. Frierson has received ACLD's President's Distinguished Service Award. He has worked extensively with exceptional children particularly in the areas of gifted and learning disabled. A family of eight, including two sets of twins, has provided many opportunities for Dr. Frierson to "practice what he preaches."

H. Stephen Glenn, Ph.D., national consultant in teacher training, education, alcoholism and drug abuse. He has been Director of the National Drug Abuse Center for Training and Resource Development in Washington, D.C. Dr. Glenn has served on many national task forces and advisory committees on Juvenile Justice, Elementary and Secondary Education, Drug Abuse and Alcoholism. He has written many papers, articles and booklets and has produced several television and film programs including an award winning educational television series on the family called "Involved".

Don Shaw, M.A., Coordinator of Health Education programs for Colorado's largest school district. He is a recipient of the Colorado "Teacher of the Year" Award, and Liberty Bell Award, and a Betty Ford Recognition Award for his work in preventative substance abuse and developing understanding of the problem. As a nationally and internationally known consultant, Mr. Shaw works with students, teachers, administrators and parents developing effective programs for teens.

ILLUSTRATOR: Paule Niedrach　　　　　GRAPHIC ARTIST: Ken Maul

American Training Center
P.O. Box 3140, High Mar Station
Boulder, CO 80307
1-(800)-365-5010

ISBN 0-911023-01-1

ACKNOWLEDGEMENTS

To acknowledge everyone who contributed to the completion of this program in so many meaningful ways would require numerous pages and we would still miss some people.

However, an extra special thanks for her expertise, support, humor and many hours of time goes to Dr. Diane "Arch" Archer, who provided the sounding board needed to critique and fine tune this program.

To Lisa Jamsa, who smoothed the rugged edges of the Handbook, my friend and colleague, thank you.

To the students at Centaurus, Fairview and West High School, who gave me ideas, adolescent perspective and the opportunity to share their thoughts with you, a special thanks for their candid comments.

To my children and Kelly, a very special "thanks", for the experiences families share, the joys and tough times we've all been through, and the love they give to me so I can share with you.

PREFACE

In the task of raising and educating our children, teachers' and parents' primary helping tool is themselves. The most critical factors in this process are the attitudes and beliefs each of us has about our role in the development of children. We decide what to do on the basis of how we perceive our role.

Knowledge seldom changes how we do things unless there is a clarification of principles or a shift in our beliefs and values. **You've Got To Be Kid-ding** has drawn together the thoughts of many "great people" in the field of human relations. These thoughts have combined the best thinking of successful people in the business, education, home, medical, psychiatric, and philosophical fields. Added to theory is the real world experience of the joys, rewards, and frustrations of raising 31 children and foster children by the featured consultants and the author.

You've Got To Be Kid-ding is not designed as a cure-all approach that works for everyone. It is designed to provide clarity for some of the age-old principles and myths assigned to child rearing. Throughout the program, ideas are presented to "shed light" on some of our current beliefs and values. History has seen child rearing "experts" proclaim the merits of strictness and control, permissiveness and "freedom of choice", and all points along the continuum from the adult-controlled to the child-centered focus.

An eclectic philosophy based upon the premise that positive discipline linked with real world consequences and the dignity of human beings, for both adults and children, pervades the thoughts of this program.

Change, created through insight and successful experience in our relationships with adolescents, may increase our chances for "growing" capable, responsible, and independent children for the future.

Learn, enjoy, and grow.

TABLE OF CONTENTS

Title Page i
Authors & Featured Consultants ii
Acknowledgements iii
Preface iv
Table of Contents v
   Program Overview ix
      Assignment Information xi
   Preprogram Questionnaire xii
   Introduction: To Participants xiv
   Parent's Prayer xvi
   Letter to Teachers and Parents xvii
   The Chick Hatches xviii
   Module I   Life Ain't Like It Used to Be! 1
      What People Want Out Of Life 3
      Four Goals of Our Culture 3
      Trends 4
      Characteristics That Lead To Good Relationships With Teens 4
      Activity/Reading Assignment 5
      The Significant Seven 5
      Whose Problem? Getting The Problem Into Perspective 6
      Well Developed Situational Skills 10
      A Teenager - What Is It? 11
      Families in Transition 14
      Developing Independent People 16
      Protective/Dependent vs. Unprotective/Independent 17
      When Teaching Children How To Do New Things 20
      Hints For Coping With Teens 20

   Module II   Paddle Your Own Canoe 21
      Teaching Responsibility 22
      To Get Kids To Accept Problems And Want To Change 22
      Rights of Parents And Teachers 23
      Elements of "Good" Schools, Classrooms And Families 23
      Elements of Effective Parenting 24
      Whose Problem Worksheet 25
      Activity/Reading Assignment 26
      Communication: A Key To Relationships 27
      Using "I" Messages Effectively 29
      Developing Strong Intrapersonal Skills 30
      Risk, The Real World and Common Sense 31
      Model Taking Care of Yourself 35
      Summary of Talks With Teens About Responsibility 35
      Grandma's Rule 37
      Adolescent Daydreaming 43
      Alternatives to "No" 45
      Cooperation and Household Chores 45

   Module III   Communication and Dialog 47
      The A-B-C of Rational Adjustment 48
      Responsibilty - What Makes It So Hard To Give? 49
      Blocks To Communication 50
      Translating "You" Messages Into "I" Messages 51

Meaning, Purpose and Significance In Life 52
Feeling Words.. 52
Activity/Reading Assignment 53
Natural and Logical Consequences 54
Logical/Natural Consequences vs. Punishment 54
Three Approaches To Discipline For Parents and Teachers 57
Natural and Logical Consequences: How Do We Know When We've Got One? 58
Teaching Good Judgement 59
Three Perceptions 60
Assertiveness 63
Family Meetings 65
Con Games... 65
Dealing With Conflict.. 66
On Telling The Truth 67
Words To Express Feelings 68

Module IV   Goof And Grow.. 71
Three Conditions For Teaching Self-Discipline And Responsibility 72
Five Traits of A Good Teacher Or Parent 73
Guided Practice Worksheet.. 74
Guide For Observers.. 75
Activity/Reading Assignment 76
The Road To Excellence 77
Listening 78
Giving Feelings Credibility 79
Developing Skills in Relationships With Others............................. 82
Grounding 83
Preparation For The Real World 84
Power Struggles.. 85
Kids Who Don't Confide 87
S/he's Never With The Family Anymore!...................................... 88
Things Adults Ask Kids To Do To Make Them Feel Listened To 88

Module V   The Kid Next Door.. 91
Communication Involves Two Major Elements.................................. 92
Good Listening Requires 92
Feelings Expressed In Gestures 93
We Disregard Teens Feelings When We: 93
We Can Attend To Kids' Feelings By:.. 94
Our Self-Image Changes Because Of:... 94
Self-Image Comes From.. 94
Observer's Worksheet... 95
Activity/Reading Assignment 96
Encouraging Self-Esteem.. 97
Praise... 98
Contracts.. 100
Adjustment As A Game Process... 104
It's Hard To Get My Kids To "Pitch In" And Help!.......................... 105
Units Of Worry 106
Giving Advice 107
Giving Effective Feedback 107

Module VI   Encouragement... 109
Meaning, Purpose, And Significance 110
The Importance Of Success 110

What Causes DisCOURAGEment? 111
The Antidote? EnCOURAGEment 111
Replacing Discouraging Statements With Encouraging Ones 113
Planning For Behavior Change 114
Contracting For Behavior Change At Home: Dialog 115
Contracting For Behavior Change At School: Dialog 117
According To Teens, A Good Parent: 118
Activity/Reading Assignment 119
Authority and Rules 120
Learning - Whose Problem? 122
Rescuing Kids 123
Kids Need To Own Their Own Feelings - And Their Own Learning! 123
The Language Of Encouragement 124
Adults Don't Change 126
Clothes 127
Winners 127

Module VII   Playing The School Game 129
Ways To Play The Games Of Life 130
Transitions In Schools 131
Teaching/Learning Models 131
Activity/Reading Assignment 132
Steps To Problem Solving 132
You Really Oughta Wanna! 136
Which TAKE Do You Want To TEST? 137
Normal Distribution Curve "Itis" 138
Additional Thoughts On Time Out 139
Additional Thoughts On Contracting 139
Skipping School 140

Module VIII   Filling Teen's Toolbox For Life 141
Creative Problem Solving Skills 142
Brainstorming 142
Mind Stretching Questions 142
Exploring Alternatives With Teens 143
Ways To Win 143
Perceptions And Skills 144
To Teach The Tools For Life To Adolescents 144
Neverending Effort 145
The Creative Teaching Style 146
Some Call It A "Higher Level Of Love" 147

Post Program Questionnaire 148
References for Further Reading & Practice 151

YOU'VE GOT TO BE KID-DING!
A LOOK AT ADOLESCENTS

Program Overview

Module I   LIFE AIN'T WHAT IT USED TO BE!

—Develop an attitude about learning new skills that allows for mistakes.
—Identify people's major goals in life.
—Understand the impact of American societal changes in the last 50 years on families, education, and adolescents.
—Increase understanding of teen rebellion.
—Identify five characteristics of an environment in which children can grow into capable people who think highly of themselves.

Module II   PADDLE YOUR OWN CANOE

—Identify when a problem belongs to kids and when it belongs to adults.
—Understand the steps involved in giving and teaching RESPONSIBILITY.
—Identify elements found in a "good" classroom or family.
—Identify your own style of teaching and disciplining teens.
—Understand the elements of an effective "teaching" and/or "parenting" style.
—Acquire at least two new ideas for dealing with teens who don't help at home.

Module III   COMMUNICATION AND DIALOG

—Understand where beliefs about things come from.
—Identify some of the beliefs adults have about their roles as Parents and Teachers.
—Identify two blocks to communication with others.
—Practice stating personal feelings in a productive way.
—Understand the benefits of feedback.
—Be able to use at least one new way to avoid Power Struggles with teens.
—Practice and be able to DIALOG more effectively with teens.

Module IV   GOOF AND GROW

- —Identify five traits of a "good" teacher or parent.
- —Understand the effect TECHNIQUE has upon the style people use in relating to classes and individuals.
- —Appreciate the gap between the age of maturity of American youth and youth in the rest of the world.
- —Understand the three requirements for teaching Self-discipline and Responsibility.
- —Understand the difference in outcome between Natural or Logical Consequences and Punishment.
- —Design Logical Consequences effectively.
- —Understand how to use a Natural or Logical Consequence to teach.

Module V   THE KID NEXT DOOR

- —Understand the elements of Good Listening.
- —Be able to respond effectively to teen "feelings" messages.
- —Understand the impact of Self-esteem on behavior and behavior change.
- —Be able to use the SCORING technique to gather information about how teens feel about themselves.
- —Be able to use information about Self-esteem to help teens change.
- —Understand the effect being "99" has on the way teens perform.

Module VI   ENCOURAGEMENT

- —Understand the difference between enCOURAGEment and disCOURAGEment.
- —Practice enCOURAGING statements.
- —Understand the relationship between success and performance.
- —Be able to differentiate between Praise and Encouragement.
- —Understand the elements of behavioral contracts and be able to apply them.

Module VII   PLAYING THE SCHOOL GAME

- —Understand the choices teens have when playing the School Game.
- —Appreciate the demands that are made upon teen's time.
- —Review the transitions in schools from the 1930s to the present.
- —Understand the impact of these transitions upon the way we teach and the way people learn.
- —Understand and experience a Teaching/Learning Model that is more likely to produce achievement and capable young people.
- —Understand whose problem learning REALLY is.
- —Provide an opportunity for adults and teens to share questions and thoughts with each other.

—Identify and be able to use four elements of "Creative" Problem Solving.
—Identify and be able to use the Steps to Problem Solving.
—Be able to use the skills necessary in Problem Solving.
—Be able to identify Five Barriers to helping teens become capable and independent.
—Be able to use Five Ways to Win with teens instead of the Five Barriers.
—Review the "Tools" teens need to become capable, independent youth.

ASSIGNMENT INFORMATION

The *Activity Assignments* are designed to provide practice in some of the skills learned during each session. Follow-up for the assignments is provided in each session to give you the opportunity to ask questions and rethink some of your ideas. If the assignments are not done, you will find that you will not have given yourself the opportunity to practice the concepts you have learned. As a result, you are more likely to have difficulty putting the concepts into practice at another time. You are more likely to forget the ideas and simply not have them available to you for future use. It is our recommendation, if you want to change some of the things you do, that you **do the assignments.**

The *Reading Assignments* are articles which will give you information that will be helpful in your discussions during the next session. We have tried providing this reading both before and after the session in which the concepts are discussed. Other participants who have completed this program suggested that they would get "a lot more out of the next session" if they have the opportunity to read about some of the ideas **before** they were presented on the film and during discussion.

The *Bonus Reading is designed to provide you with additional information about some of the concepts that are presented during your sessions and some concepts that are not presented at that time. These articles are "optional" reading.*

Tips to Use Tomorrow are additional ideas presented in an easy-to-read format. They are designed as ideas you can put into practice **tomorrow.** Again, the material may or may not be discussed during a session. Certainly, if you have questions, you will want to bring them up during your class meetings. Tips to Use Tomorrow is "optional" reading.

Module I Leader's Materials
PREPROGRAM QUESTIONNAIRE

*Adapted from materials used in Boulder Valley Schools. Original source unknown.

This questionnaire will give you a measure of your growth from the beginning to the end of your sessions in **YOU'VE GOT TO BE KID-DING!** Mark your level of comfort or skill with an X. Connect the Xs with lines to create your profile. You will be given your profile again at the end of the sessions. You will be able to chart your progress at that time.

DESIRED SKILLS	PRESENT LEVEL OF COMPETENCE					
	Inadequate —			Adequate +		
I can list at least five changes in the way families operated from 1930 to the present.	3	2	1	1	2	3
I can list at least five characteristics of a family or school environment that lead to the development of capable young people.	3	2	1	1	2	3
I know how to identify "who owns a problem" and how to leave the problem with its "owner".	3	2	1	1	2	3
I know how to teach children Responsibility, Self-control, and Self-discipline.	3	2	1	1	2	3
I know and understand the elements necessary for adolescents to feel Capable.	3	2	1	1	2	3
I am comfortable with my methods for establishing a learning environment in my classroom.	3	2	1	1	2	3
I know and use methods for disciplining teens that encourage motivation, cooperation, and achievement.	3	2	1	1	2	3
I communicate my classroom needs and feelings effectively to my students.	3	2	1	1	2	3
I feel I use good listening skills when talking with teens.	3	2	1	1	2	3
I understand the difference between the learning outcomes of punishment and natural or logical consequences.	3	2	1	1	2	3
I feel that I use effective consequences that maintain firmness, dignity, and respect for myself and teens.	3	2	1	1	2	3
I feel that I use effective methods of encouragement with adolescents.	3	2	1	1	2	3
I know the elements necessary to give Meaning, Purpose, and Significance in people's lives.	3	2	1	1	2	3
I understand the effects of self-esteem on adolescent behavior.	3	2	1	1	2	3
I create a learning environment where self-esteem is nurtured.	3	2	1	1	2	3

I understand the elements of an effective behavioral contract and can apply them.

3　2　1　　1　2　3

My approach to teaching is effective in producing learners who achieve well within their individual limits and feel capable.

3　2　1　　1　2　3

I understand ideas teens have about their lives, goals, priorities, and experiences from their point of viewing.

3　2　1　　1　2　3

I can teach adolescents to be effective decision makers and problem solvers.

3　2　1　　1　2　3

I know and understand the perceptions teens must have about themselves in order to function well as adults.

3　2　1　　1　2　3

I know and understand the basic skills people must have in order to function effectively in a democratic system.

3　2　1　　1　2　3

I understand the elements and importance of Dialog and can use it effectively.

3　2　1　　1　2　3

Adolescence is a time in children's lives, looked forward to by youth and seldom understood by adults. Teachers, administrators, parents -- are continually challenged to come up with the "right" approach to teenagers. The result can be uncertainty, confusion, guilt, anger, frustration, and a sense of failure. While educators spend years learning to "teach" youth, few of us, either professionals or parents have any guidelines for raising "capable adolescents" except the memories of our own experiences as teens and the wisdom we gain from trial and error.

In the past, families (parents, aunts, uncles, grandparents, cousins, and old friends) joined in the job of "growing" capable young people. However, since the early 1950s, this support has all but vanished.

The management of children's behavior has been a concern in our schools for several decades. As the responsibility for teaching social skills has been added to the traditional school program of academic subjects, curriculum has had to adjust to teaching children the ability to respond appropriately to others, to relate effectively, and to be responsible. Parents and educators, recognizing limitations in their abilities to teach these skills and the resulting frustrations of the teen years, have searched for ways to deal with these issues. We want children in our care to be happy, successful and learn the skills necessary for living in the adult world.

You've Got To Be Kid-ding! is designed to help you "take another look" at the relationships between teenagers and themselves. You, will explore many ideas.

It will be important for you to understand that some of the ideas may not fit your values and life style. You will need to ask yourself:

-Which of these ideas makes sense for me to try?
-What are some of the ways that I will be able to learn new skills - without seeming too phony and without throwing away my personal beliefs and values?
-How should I practice these new skills?

"Don't fix what isn't broken!" is most applicable whenever we are trying to improve anything. The ideas, information, and approaches suggested in **You've Got To Be Kid-ding!** have worked at one time or another for someone else. They are presented for your consideration to use with kids when what is being done isn't working.

As we reviewed reactions from those who have participated in this program, the major concern was that so many ideas, strategies and successful approaches are presented that people become frustrated, feeling that they should be doing all things at once. It seems to be human nature to want to do things perfectly and immediately. However, we know that change doesn't happen that way. It requires practice, time and often includes mistakes. Just as you will learn to remember this concept as you work with kids, keep it in mind for yourself. We are often our own worst critics.

Allow for mistakes and then ask yourself:

> -Have I done the best I could given what I knew at the time? If the answer is yes, then ask the next question.
> -Will I be able to do better next time given what I have learned?

The distance traveled to create change and promote excellence is often so much longer than we originally suspected. Give yourself time and be patient.

RULES FOR LEARNING

Following these rules will diminish the stress you might feel and provide an enjoyable environment in which both you and your teenagers can grow and learn together. Refer to them periodically throughout the program.

> 1. As you consider techniques and approaches presented, don't feel you have to use every one of them. Choose those that are most comfortable for you - those that fit your values and beliefs. Try them on, like new clothes and if they don't fit, discard them!
>
> 2. Work on ONE thing at a time! We have a tendency to want the "whole" problem to be solved at once. Success usually comes more readily when one issue is resolved at a time. Pick the one that will make the biggest DIFFERENCE to your relationship in the SHORTEST AMOUNT OF TIME.
>
> 3. Practice with friends! Often we pick a "life or death" situation to try out new approaches or skills. If you were driving a car for the first time, would you pick an instructor who criticized you, refused to teach you if you didn't do it perfectly, and allowed NO mistakes? Teens can be our friends, if we let them know we are practicing a new way of doing things. Spouses can be friends, when they are learning too.
>
> 4. Set realistic expectations for yourself. Learning new ways is like breaking in a new pair of shoes. They are a bit uncomfortable and don't feel exactly the way we want them to, at first.
>
> 5. Find someone who will support you, while you are learning. Look around this class, you may find someone here.
>
> If you knew you couldn't fail—
> What would you do then?

A PARENT'S PRAYER

Oh, heavenly Father, make me a better parent. Teach me to understand my children, to listen patiently to what they have to say, and to answer all their questions kindly. Keep me from interrupting them or contradicting them. Make me as courteous to them as I would have them be to me. Forbid that I should ever laugh at their mistakes, or resort to shame or ridicule when they displease me. May I never punish them for my own selfish satisfaction or to show my power.

Let me not tempt my child to lie or steal. And guide me hour by hour that I may demonstrate by all I say and do that honesty produces happiness.

Reduce, I pray, the meanness in me. And when I am out of sorts, help me, Oh Lord, to hold my tongue.

May I ever be mindful that my children are children and I should not expect of them the judgment of adults.

Let me not rob them of the opportunity to wait on themselves and to make decisions.

Bless me with the bigness to grant them all their reasonable requests, and the courage to deny them privileges I know will do them harm.

Make me fair and just and kind. And fit me, Oh Lord, to be loved and respected and imitated by my children.

Amen.

Author unknown.
This prayer was found in an old family Bible.

To Teachers and Parents and others who may be concerned about children,

I would like to share my concerns about the directions being set in many High Schools today.

Recent statistics concerning the academic standards of our secondary schools indicate that not only do our students achieve lower scores on national tests than they did ten years ago, they don't compete favorably today with students in the rest of the world!

The business community's focus on **excellence,** as described in Thomas J. Peters' book, *In Search of Excellence,* has filtered through to application in many educational institutions. Our students are not adequately prepared for the "high tech" society in which they must live.

I firmly believe that we need a well-defined, concerted effort to increase academic achievement and pursue **EXCELLENCE** in our educational process.

My concern lies with **how** this improvement takes place. Will our zeal for mechanical competence with computers, increased skills in math and science, and improvement in writing mechanics make us forget the humanness of the students for whom the programs are designed? Will we reward mechanical and technical skills at the expense of thinking skills? Will we *require* **perfection** rather than *encourage* **excellence?**

John Naisbitt, in his best seller, *Megatrends,* says that "high touch" needs to be a major focus in our "high tech" society. **What** is taught must be balanced by **how** it is taught! The how of teaching involves the process for transferring the learning. It also involves the **relationship** between the *teacher* and *learner.*

The purpose for this program is to combine the "high tech" of teaching with the "high touch" of learning. It contains both the elements necessary for good teaching and the feelings necessary for good learning.

Stephen Glenn tells us that we find meaning and purpose in our lives by:

1. Being listened to and understood.

2. Being taken seriously as a human being.

3. Being genuinely needed.

If learning in our schools and families is to lead to meaning in our children's lives, and **democracy** in our country's future, we *must* not only fill kids' heads, but fill their hearts and meet their needs as human beings. We must teach about the **real** world with firmness *and* with dignity and respect.

This job of "growing capable young people" is a grave responsibility for parents, teachers, administrators, and boards of education. My charge to you is to take on that challenge and carry it forward. The future depends on it!!

Respectfully,

Helen Ryley

THE CHICK HATCHES

Did you ever watch a chick hatch from an egg? The first attempts are meek peckings from the inside. Then a crack begins to form. The observer senses a struggle for the chick's very existence. The pecking goes on and on. So much energy is spent. And then - nothing. The observer's tension increases. The plexiglass over the incubator prevents any help. The warmth and safety of the incubator provide the environment, but the chick must find a way to emerge on its own.

Another crack begins on the other side. "Oh! Why didn't you keep going with the crack that you had started!" And so goes the struggle - for hours. Eventually, the cracks find a way to fall together. A hole grows bigger and given the time, strength, and the continued support of the environment, a chick emerges - faltering, wet, and ready to take its place in the world. Nature provides support for a short while longer and then the chick is on its own to survive or perish.

The trials and tribulations, joys and excitement, anxiety and support involved in the emergence of adolescents from childhood to adults is much like the struggle of the chick.

As adults - teachers, parents, relatives, concerned friends - we observe the struggle of our teens. We may even remember our own "highs and lows" from that period in our lives. Wanting to help more than the "plexiglass" will allow creates stresses in our lives. Adolescence is a time to "get through".

And yet, the teen years can sparkle with delight. To watch a child emerge - discover his or her identity, strengths, values, potential - is a joy. If we can laugh with our children about the mistakes, if we can maintain a balance of love, influence, inspiraton, and independence, if we can remain open and available when really needed, we'll know the effort is worth it. Today's adolescents are the future!

MODULE 1
LIFE AIN'T WHAT IT USED TO BE!

Gem

Happiness is: Feeling Successful

You will find **gems of wisdom** throughout this program. They represent thoughts, ideas, and statements from the program's authors. They may prove to be helpful "memory hooks" - or reminders for you as you put the program concepts into practice.

Gem

Success and Failure = What we believe about what we are told!

Gem

I don't become what I think I can,
I don't become what you think I can,
I become what I think you think I can.

****

Mistakes are one of the most important ways we **learn!**

****

WHAT PEOPLE WANT OUT OF LIFE

—To be **happy**

—To be **loved**

—To be **important**

—To have a little **variety**

****

Happiness is a major goal in life.

Love and Feelings of **Success** = **Happiness.**

****

FOUR GOALS OF OUR CULTURE

1. Work
2. School
3. Get married
4. Have kids

TRENDS

1. Achievement dropped.

2. Rising incidence of: violent crime
   suicide
   drug and alcohol abuse
   pregnancy

3. Changes in Lifestyle — moved from rural to urban society.

4. Jump in birth rate in 1946 (after World War II).

5. Change in educational approaches. Twenty times the number of kids in school in 1951.

****

Healthy Teens Are Ones Who Decide or Choose.

****

CHARACTERISTICS THAT LEAD TO GOOD RELATIONSHIPS WITH TEENS

1. Adults send messages that they expect kids **can** do what they need to and do their best.

2. Adults and kids **feel good about themselves.**

3. Teens make most of the **decisions** about things that affect them personally.

4. The focus is on **successes.**

5. Teens experience the **consequences** (including mistakes) of their decisions in order to learn.

****

Each of us needs to feel **important.**

ACTIVITY ASSIGNMENT

Select a teen upon whom you would like to focus throughout this program. You will probably be thinking of that person in terms of some of the "problems" the two of you have. During the week, think about the relationship. Each time you think of something that makes you enjoy and appreciate the relationship, write it down in the space below. Be prepared to share these good things at the next session.

READING ASSIGNMENT

HANDBOOK pp. 5-11 (This reading will prepare you for the next session.)

"The Significant Seven" by Stephen Glenn
"Whose Problem? Getting the Problem into Perspective"
"Well-Developed Situational Skills" by Stephen Glenn

Bonus Reading

HANDBOOK pp. 11-19 (This reading supplements today's session topics.)

"A Teenager - What Is It?"
"Families in Transition" by Stephen Glenn
"Developing Independent People" by Stephen Glenn
"Protective/Dependent vs. Nonprotective/Independent"

Tips to Use Tomorrow

HANDBOOK pp. 20 (These are ideas you can put into use tomorrow.)

"When Teaching Children How to Do New Things"
"Hints for Coping with Teens"

There is something very special about the teen years. When teachers and parents feel they have the skills to deal with teens, this time can be an enriching and gratifying experience for both adults and teens.

THE SIGNIFICANT SEVEN Stephen Glenn

We need to talk about the special skills people need and use to become happy and capable. Most theorists agree that people need to feel good about themselves to be happy. Unfortunately, a discussion of the importance of a positive self-concept or high self-esteem does little to explain **how** a person develops self-esteem. It does little good to say that a child who misbehaves lacks self-esteem. The diagnosis itself is not the cure.

We have seen too many parents, teachers, and school administrators receive a diagnosis of a child's problem without being given the least idea of how the problem can be solved. This leads to frustration and a feeling of helplessness on the part of the parent or teacher. The lack of practical knowledge and the lack of an idea of what to do has made many parents withdraw from the problem. They think that there is nothing which **can** be done, and therefore, ignoring the problem is less painful than continually failing at attempts to correct it.

A person who learns to believe in his own ability to solve problems, rather than waiting for some outside cure, increases his ability to handle the situations in which he finds himself. Similarly, as he recognizes problems and develops the situational skills, his judgmental ability increases. He feels better about himself and, as his self-esteem increases, his ability to solve his own problems also blossoms.

Competence in seven significant perceptions and skills is necessary to the development of a strong and capable individual. Underdevelopment in these areas leads to behavioral patterns which cause problems for the individual and for society.

Perceptions and Skills

We have identified seven basic perceptions and skills which are necessary for teenagers to develop if they are to become successful, independent people.

Perceptions:

1. I am **capable.**

2. I **contribute in meaningful ways** and I am **genuinely needed.**

3. I can **influence what happens to me.**

Four Skills:

1. Strong **intrapersonal** skills. The ability to talk *within yourself* about what happens, why it happens, and what effects occur. The ability to be self-disciplined, self-controlled, and learn from experiences.

2. Strong **interpersonal** skills. The ability to communicate *with others* to develop friendships, establish deep human relationships, and validate our identity.

3. Strong **situational** skills. The ability to respond to the limits and requirements in situations we meet in our everyday life - responsibility, adaptability, and flexibility to meet situational needs with intent and integrity.

4. Good **judgmental** skills. Wisdom and comprehension of relationships in our environment.

These attitudes and skills are discussed throughout **You've Got To Be Kid-ding.**

WHOSE PROBLEM? GETTING THE PROBLEM INTO PERSPECTIVE

The bottom line for most teachers and parents is the feeling that they are responsible for the way things turn out. Not so! In fact, when we are having trouble with our teen we are probably:

1. Making our own life unhappy and adding to its stresses.

2. Trying to run our teen's life.

Unfortunately, adults can not insure success for children. In fact, it becomes harder to influence the outcome of events in children's lives as they get older. The only sure way to impact children's lives as they grow toward adulthood is to give them many opportunities to deal with the **choices and consequences** they meet along the way. Every time we solve our children's problems, we rob them of a learning opportunity. We send the message that they aren't capable and can't succeed without our help.

When parents are loving and achieving, there is one issue that creates most parent/child friction -parents' lack of ability to make a distinction between their child's problems and their own problems. This confusion carries over into school. A teacher, concerned about a student's academic success, will call the parents, hoping that pressure from home *and* school will "make" the student improve his or her grades. Sometimes it works, particularly if the student is used to letting others do the thinking and deciding for him. Other times, the student figures "If you're going to worry, I don't have to," or "Make me!"

Think of a teenager.

Make a list of all the things that your teen does that bother you.

Some parents and teachers cite the following problems with teens:

Doesn't do homework.
Swears.
Ties up the phone for hours.
Smokes pot.
Won't do chores.
Stays up late.
Says homework is finished when it isn't.
Talks to friends when he or she should be working.
Leaves wet towels all over the bathroom.
Has an older boyfriend.
Watches too much TV.
Gets girlfriend pregnant.
Won't clean up his or her room.
Won't go to school.
Late for class regularly.
Not enough money to buy gas for car to get to school - spent it on fun.
Used my car and left gas tank empty.
Demands money.
Up for a scholarship but lets grades slip.

These lists of problems can be divided into three groups:

1. The **teen's** problem
2. **My** problem
3. **Our** problem

Where would you put them? Where would you put those on your list?

THE TEENS	MINE	OURS
Problem does not affect parent's (teacher's) life, now or in the future.	Problem affects parent (teacher) personally.	Problem is really the teen's but the parent (teacher) is the responsible adult.
Makes bad grades.	Makes noise (from fights and tantrums).	Runs away from home.
		Throws tantrums.
Listens to loud music.	Drops out of school before age 16.	
Gets girlfriend pregnant.	Swears.	Behaves dangerously in school.
Doesn't do homework.	Keeps pot in the house.	Behaves dangerously on school bus.
Is late for class regularly.	Interrupts "private" time.	
Fights with sister or brother.		
Won't do things with the family.		

If you're having trouble deciding where a problem should be listed, ask yourself if you have any real control over the situation. If you control part of the situation the problem is probably "ours".

Some teen problems which affect our lives:

—Fights with brothers and sisters.

  * Noise affects me. Kids can continue fighting outside.

—Watches too much TV.

  * Prevents me from watching my TV programs. Agree on when I choose programs.

— Has "undesirable" friends.

   * "Friends" come to my house against my wishes. May have friends but not at my house. May have to lock doors when gone.

— Doesn't do homework.

   * Affects me when it disturbs the rest of the class while they are doing homework. Student may stay quietly or leave.

— Is failing your class.

   * Administration sees student failure as a "poor teaching" problem. Contracting for behavior change at least gives a paper trail.

— Has just taken a dive off the balcony into the senior locker area and hits his head on one of the lockers.

   * School's problem (and therefore mine) since I am responsible for the safety of students. Dives may be taken, but not here!

— A student walks into class stoned.

   * Deciding to use or not to use drugs is a student problem. Availability and or use in school is a school problem. Drugs, themselves, are a societal problem and quite complex.

If you've decided to give your teen the responsibility for his or her own problems, drop the urge to mold the situation.

Try asking yourself:

   1. Can I control the outcome of this situation - really?

   2. Can I control part of the outcome? I can't control when she goes to sleep but I can wake her up! (Leads to a very natural consequence - TIRED!)

   3. What can I do that would contribute to this teen's being more responsible and capable in making his or her own decisions?

Developing trust that teens can and will make the right decisions is tough. However, if you continue to take the responsibility for their problems, they aren't going to have the opportunity to learn.

When you give responsibilities back to teens, behavior may get worse before it gets better. It's a bit of a shock when the teen has to "go it alone". He or she may try to get you to go back to your "old way". You may see temper tantrums. You may get "You don't care about me anymore" statements.

Persevere! The outcome will be a person who feels and is more capable! And there's more good news. You'll be taking better care of yourself, relinquishing your guilt, lowering your stress, and moving toward a better relationship with the teens in your life.

How Do I Start This Change?

1. Pick out **one** responsibility to give back to your teen. (One that won't be too hard for you to relinquish since you want to insure your success!)

2. Tell the teen you are returning the responsibility to him or her using an "I" statement. Rehearse the statement. Make it short and clear. Include what **you** are going to do without telling the teen what he or she could or should do. Say it **without anger, in a moment of calm.** If you are angry, it is probably still your problem.

3. Give a "Good Luck" message which says you're rooting for success, whatever that may be. You have confidence he or she will handle the situation, and while you will always be interested and available for consultation, the problem is no longer yours.

EXAMPLES:

"Colleges usually require average or better grades for entrance. Good luck!"

"As we agreed, I provide 'good student' auto insurance. The insurance bill is due in about 30 days. Good luck!" (Avoid the temptation to add "and I'm not paying the extra!")

Parents and teachers say that resolving the **whose problem** issue relieves a lot of pressure on the relationship. It can also lead to concern as adults watch teens "try out their new wings". Protective adults have to try on a whole new image - unprotected, loving - just as their teens are doing. It's not easy!!

Capable people develop from children who expect to solve their own problems. If they have seen adults model taking care of themselves and taking responsibility for their own problems, teens are much more likely to act that way, too. Good luck!

WELL-DEVELOPED SITUATIONAL SKILLS Stephen Glenn

Throughout your reading, you will come across articles clarifying the three perceptions and four skills of the Significant Seven that you read about on pp. 5-6. This article leads into some ideas you will discuss in Module II.

There are **limits** and **expectations** which make certain behavior acceptable and certain other behavior unacceptable. **Learning to recognize the limits** inherent in a situation is the first step in acquiring good situational skills.

Once we recognize the situation for what it is, we then need to be able to take the responsibility to respond positively to the limits and adapt our behavior so that there are constructive results. Three aspects - recognition, responsibility, and adaptabilty - form the core of situational skills. People who possess these skills successfully handle a wide variety of circumstances and fit comfortably into a multitude of situations.

Weaknesses in these skills often lead people to refuse to accept the consequences of their behavior. Rather than face their own behavior and its logical or natural outcomes, they are likely to blame "the system" for their difficulties.

Maturity, on the other hand, comes when a person learns to look at a situation, figure out what behavior best fits the situation (that is, what behavior will result in desirable outcomes), and adapts to that situation. This does not imply that all our actions and values should be situationally defined. We cannot be chameleons, adapting to any shade or hue we happen to land upon. We must act with intent and integrity. Maturity in situational skills is knowing how to associate consequences with decisions and actions and knowing what is required in a given situation.

BONUS READING

A TEENAGER — WHAT IS IT?

"Teenager" is a title given to that period of time in a youngster's life after childhood and before adulthood. In primitive cultures this passing from child to adult is done ceremoniously with no real social accommodation for the transition. Today, we designate a period in children's lives when they are no longer "children" and not yet "adult" and we call it "adolescence". Then we muddy the water by treating teenagers as "adults" (adult fares at movies) and as children ("R" rated - parents must be along). As a result, teens and adults become confused about expectations.

In primitive societies maturity was assumed. Adulthood was accomplished upon completion of the tribal test and rituals. In our society, no one is sure about the criteria for adulthood, let alone when we reach it. Some of us never accomplish the task!

In 1979, the World Health Organization studied the process of young people's development into fully functioning adults. Functional adulthood is defined as that point in a person's life when he or she becomes responsible for his or her own behavior, well-being and, if necessary, support. The average young person living in an urbanized, technologically advanced nation other than the United States, reaches functional adulthood between the ages of 16 and 17. In the United States, this maturation process continues into the early 20's! The major factor limiting the maturation process is **dependency**!

What needs to happen to help our young people become capable, sooner? **You've Got To Be Kid-ding** has many thoughts for accomplishing this.

Stages Of Adolescence

Several stages of growth have been identified by developmental psychologists as part of the time in life known as adolescence. Teens experience major physical, emotional, and cognitive changes during the years from 11 to 18. With these changes come some fairly consistent behaviors and needs.

Pre-Adolescence

Pre-adolescence (11-13) is, developmentally, a stage in which the task is to reorganize from patterns of childhood to those of adulthood. This means **trying on** many emotions, values, approaches to tasks and adults, and discovery of which ones will lead them toward *their* goals of independence and self-worth.

According to Dr. Fitzhugh Dodson, the pre-adolescent years tend to be difficult for adults and kids. Behavior labeled obnoxious by adults is the style of the young teen as he or she remodels or just plain throws away the ways of childhood. The development of autonomy is comparable to that same struggle in a two-year-old.

Dr. Foster Cline describes adolescents as "two-year-olds with hormones and wheels" in his book, *Parent Text*. Since two-year-olds are still little we can impose our will fairly successfully. Not so with adolescents!

Early Adolescence

During early adolescence (13-15), teens are trying to answer the question "Who am I?". They are also coping with an entirely new set of feelings - sexual urges. Body changes further confuse the "Who am I?" issue. Mixed with the search for independence and lack of emotional confidence, this time of life becomes one of testing families, teachers, schools, friends, rules, etc. Adults' biggest mistake is to take this testing, this rebellion, personally.

Teacher: That kind of behavior is not accepted in my classroom. I am going to ask you to leave until you can cool down and return to do the work I asked you to do.

Sally: That's not fair! It's stupid to have to rewrite the whole paper 'cause there are a few scratched out words in it!

Teacher: Sally, you're really upset. (Dealing with the feelings -not the content.)

Sally: I sure am! I spent all last night writing this .....paper!

Teacher: Please leave until you can cool down. You can go to my office until you feel less angry. Then we'll discuss rewriting your paper. See you as soon as you're ready.

Sally: Oh, all right! I'm going. But I still don't see what you've got against a few scratched out words. It's just not fair.

Note: The wise teacher will say no more. Sally's doing what the teacher asked. Her parting comments are not directed at the teacher but at the focus of the original anger.

Dealing with the feelings behind the outbursts instead of the actual content helps deflect the attack and says you are trying to understand. **Open channels of communication** with emotional support are key in a continuing relationship between adults and teens. A skeleton of limits, values, and "asked for" advice provides a secure framework within which the child can grow, make choices and mistakes, and try on the "new me".

More and more responsibility for the youth's life is passing from the adults to the child. Relationships built on mutual respect rather than the power of adult authority will work to the satisfaction of the teen and the adult.

Later Adolescence

As the adolescent reaches the late teen years (16+), the issues of independence and family/peer group identity fade, to be replaced by the search for a more global identity. Within the larger framework of society, the youth must make decisions about:

1. Vocational direction
2. Satisfactory sexual relationships
3. Future love and family life
4. Complete independence from parents and the family life of his or her childhood

By this time the adolescent has not only the "hormones", he or she also has wheels!

It is not within our reach to control our teen's life problems. It is within our reach to meet our own needs in relation to that teen. Curfew is a good example.

At six o'clock one Saturday evening, Tami, 16, left for a picnic at a local park saying, "I'm not sure what time I'll be home, but it shouldn't be late."

Her Mom was comfortable with that information until about 11:00 when she began to worry. "What if something happened to her?"

Midnight came and went.

At 12:30, Tami came in saying, "You're still up, Mom?"

"Yes, I was worried about you. I'm not usually a worrier but it just didn't make sense to me that a picnic would last this long."

"I'm sorry. I took a whole bunch of kids home and we stopped to joke around with Jane's folks for about an hour."

"My problem is that sometime you might need my help to get you out of a tough spot. As much as I try not to think about kidnaps, rapes, and such, they do happen. Or your car might have broken down again. I had no idea where or when to begin to help you - if you had needed me."

"I guess I should have called."

"I would appreciate that. It will save my worrying and might help you some day if you'll keep me more informed."

FAMILIES IN TRANSITION Stephen Glenn

There was a time in America when the attitudes, values, and behavior of each generation were effectively passed on to the next generation as the natural result of interaction between parents and children. By the time a boy reached the teenage years, if his parents were infirm or had died, he could step in and fill his father's role because he had been actively associated with it from infancy. In a similar way, a girl learned to take over her mother's role. At age 16 or 17, there were very few mysteries about being an adult and being part of the adult world. In 1935, this traditional pattern existed for seventy percent of all Americans.

Rural Lifestyle

The lifestyle was essentially rural. The typical pattern of interaction from family to family was the pattern of working together. A child would often work ten hours of the day alongside one or both of his parents. Almost from the time he or she was old enough to walk and speak he was there - solving problems, watching decisions being made, making decisions, learning about values, getting on-the-job training. He or she was a participant and not just an observer in the adult world.

There remained about six waking hours after the day's work was done. Some of this time was spent eating, and mealtime was very much a discussion time. Evening hours were also spent learning handicrafts, making clothing or things actually used in the home or for work. Children sang, played, and learned to read and write. There was much interaction between brothers and sisters, parents and children - all the family members, often including grandparents.

Extended Families

Living in an extended family also had important consequences. Aunts, uncles, cousins, and grandparents were close at hand.

If Dad came down on you very heavily, Grandma was there to say, "He was like that when he was a boy, too. But you had better go along and do what he says."

In this way even the heaviest authoritarian discipline was rationalized and personalized for the child with the result that he could understand it and accept it more easily. An authoritarian discipline system was possible because there were other adults to help it become understood.

In addition, everyone had chores of their own besides the routine farm work. These chores were important personal responsibilities. If the child assigned to do the milking forgot to milk the cow for three days, the family went without milk until the cow had another calf. There were times when one had to give up doing what he wanted to do and go pull weeds. This was not busy work. If one did not pull the weeds, in three months there were no vegetables to eat. If one left home on a weekend, enough hay, water, and feed for stock and pets had to be arranged. If the three-year-old forgot to gather the eggs one evening, everybody discussed with the child the importance of not having fried eggs or an omelette for breakfast. Responsibilities began early and increased as the family members themselves grew.

In the environment of that period, there was what would now be termed a great surplus of significant interaction within the family. Because of that, no one worried about developing capable people. It just happened. It could be assumed that a child born in a home and growing up there would be like his or her parents.

The rural population had very limited access to information. Some parents had ambitions beyond the farm for their children, but they could not afford private tutors. Parents formed groups, pooled resources, and "invented" schools. In the schools, persons of all ages met together to be taught to read and write by a teacher who was carefully selected by several parents. Quite naturally these parents chose a teacher whose values and behavior were in harmony with their own.

Home/School Partnership

Together, these two institutions, the home and the school, in partnership, had the job of preparing individuals for successful living. The chief problems at that time, in view of the inadequacy of communication and the shortage of information, were illiteracy and a general isolation from world events on the part of the rural population. The school's job was to try to correct those two deficiencies. It was a lifestyle in which growing capable young people was a natural result of constant on-the-job training for adulthood.

Changes in Life Style

Between 1935 and 1950, the greatest social change ever known in this country took place in an incredible fifteen years time.

Urban Setting

By 1950, according to the census, seventy percent of all Americans lived in an urban environment, and only thirty percent on farms - a complete reversal of the 1935 statistic! By 1970, ninety percent of all Americans lived in an urban development, and even those living in a rural environment lived an urban life style. They commuted to work, had television, etc. Thus, in just thirty-five years Americans made the transition which had taken nearly 400 years in Europe.

Nuclear Families

In 1930, a child spent three to four hours per day personally involved with various members of the extended family, parents and children plus grandparents, aunts, uncles, cousins, etc., most of whom resided close by. This involvement included working together, discussion with other generations and play which required personal and imaginative interaction. Today's typical youngster has a very different experience. For most, the extended family has been reduced to what we now call the nuclear family, one or two parents plus the children. Grandparents, aunts, uncles, etc., now typically reside far away.

Within nuclear families with two parents present, interaction was reduced to fourteen and one-half minutes per day. Of these fourteen and one-half minutes, over twelve were used in one-way negatively toned communicatons - parents issuing warnings or reproaching children for things done wrong! Unbelieveable, but too true! Consider the impact of this rapid social transition on the amount and quality of family interaction alone. There was an enormous change. Urbanization virtually eliminated the likelihood that a child would work for any significant portion of this time alongside either of his parents.

Technological Change and Television

Then, in the 1940's, a technological innovation was introduced that was destined to have massive social impact. This invention was television. Television, with all its good effects, has also brought into the average home, attitudes, values, and behaviors completely foreign to those exhibited by the parents. Television is a tremendous influence in the home as a source of attitudes, values, and behaviors. Whether the children accept or adopt them or not, they are made aware of them.

Of greater significance is the fact that TV has become the hub of social and leisure time in our society. In 1970, the average American watched television for five hours per day.

If work time, sleep time, and viewing time average 23 hours of the day in a family, there is just one hour in twenty-four left for family interaction. This leaves out mealtimes and the normal business of the family. But Americans are ingenious! They discovered mealtime and viewing time could be combined. This is done at the expense of all the discussion and sharing that used to take place at the dinner table. If a family diligently uses the remaining hour every day for meaningful interaction, that results in fifteen minutes per day of interaction time for any two members of a five-member family - not a tremendous amount!

In less than thirty years we have gone from a society with a huge surplus of significant interactions between the generations, particularly within the primary family unit, to a society in which there is a critical shortage of that kind of significant interaction.

A Broad Scope of Transitions

In 1930, children grew up in on-the-job training for adulthood, actively involved in the relevant activities on which their lives depended. Today, they are not even observers of most of them. In 1930, the average child grew up surrounded by a small group of people whose values and behaviors directly reinforced those he was expected to acquire. Today, he grows up surrounded by radically different values fifteen feet in either direction from his home, and he has six different sets at school each day.

The changes which the family has undergone have been so dramatic and so rapid that family patterns have been unable to accommodate them; hence, traditional child learning processes no longer take place.

Parents and teachers need to understand two things: First, know why they no longer take place in the time honored ways and second, understand the principals of developing capable children.

Teachers and parents can then plan the kinds of activities that will help their teens reach the developmental goals. This is not accomplished in doing the same old things the same old way. It is found in respecting the principles by which human beings become capable and being sure that those are addressed today.

DEVELOPING INDEPENDENT PEOPLE Stephen Glenn

The mechanisms the family has traditionally used to develop life skills in young people no longer appear to be working as effectively as they did in the past. Along with the impact of change and the effects of reduced interaction time in the families of the 1980s, questions are being raised about the processes we have traditonally used to develop strong, independent people.

We have found that many societal problems reflect the same set of issues. People who are chronically dependent on alcohol or drugs in their lives are very much the same as those who are chronically dependent on crimes, delinquency, and vandalism. They are very much like those who are chronically dependent on the educational system (they express it by underachievement, absenteeism, or disciplinary referrals). They are very much like the chronically dependent, unemployable person.

The behavior we see is **dependency** - the inability to manage the freedom and resources available to us in our socioeconomic system. Until we approach the problem of dependency as a type of behavior, it is not possible to solve the range of specific problems which are actually different manifestations of the larger problem of dependency.

Dependency - Independence

"What causes dependence?" The answer is "Birth". We are born dependent. We all have the potential to become independent, but it takes two things to accomplish it. The first is time. The second is a series of developmental experiences, usually provided in the home and school, which help the person learn the skills of independent living.

What causes dependence is really the wrong question. The real question is: "What has not yet happened to help these people become capable?"

The profile of chronically dependent people is one of inadequate skill development, lack of attitudes leading to capabilities, and a lack of understanding of the person's place in the world in relation to other people and situations.

The family traditionally has provided experiences which greatly aid a young person in preparing for life. Technology and urbanization have altered the family's ability to provide these experiences.

PROTECTIVE/DEPENDENT VS. UNPROTECTIVE/INDEPENDENT

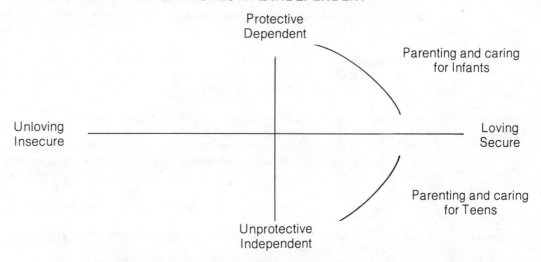

Parents (and teachers) approach parenting somewhere along these lines. While teens should be moving toward independence, high schools generally have more rules about being excused when tardy or absent, getting parent permission, etc. than grade schools. Homes have more rules and controls for their adolescents (where they go, when they come in, who they're with, and what they're doing) than they did for their kindergartners. Why is it? Because decisions are now potentially life threatening! Loving parents want the best for their kids. The problem is "How To Accomplish This?"

Babies enter the world in need of love and protection. They are dependent. Adults also need love but need to be independent, capable people who can take care of themselves. Parents, teachers, and school systems must help kids move from being Dependent (in need of protection) to Independent, (able to thrive in a nonprotective environment).

The problem with compliant and dependent little kids is when they reach about 13 they will change. Peers become more important than parents. Kids who don't think for themselves, tend to listen to and do what their peers do. They may also become very rebellious and resistant at home. Parents used to tell them what to do. Now others do!

Can Teens Think for Themselves?

One of the frustrations of living with our teenagers has been the number of dumb questions they ask:

"What time is it?"

"Do I dial 1 for long distance?"

"How do I fix the starter in my car?"

Or just the steady lack of information or misinformation about:

"When's the football banquet?"

"What are you supposed to bring to the potluck?"

And on and on. After checking with other parents, I now know lots of kids between 13 and 17 who give their parents the impression they couldn't think if they had to.

Real world: they can think if they *have* to. If you want to find out for sure, listen to your friends and teachers as they describe your child's behavior when you aren't around. What you see at home isn't all there is!

If we have given children lots of opportunities to make decisions, dialog about the goofs and the choices they will have next time;

If we have encouraged children to "think for themselves" and take care of themselves;

If we have encouraged creativity and expected independent thinking;

Our children will become capable people who can **listen to themselves** with confidence.

EXAMPLES:

Mom: "When kids are out in the street and cars are coming - do the cars stop? Sometimes not! And what happens to kids if the cars don't stop?"

Three-year-old: "They get squished?"

Mom: "Uh hum. And then what happens?"

Three-year-old: "They die?"

Mom: "Yes, and we would be very sad if you weren't here anymore."

Three-year-old: "I think I'll play in the backyard."

Mom: "Glad to hear it. Good thinking."

****

Troy: "I think I'll go down to the mall after the late movie, okay?"

Mom: "Well, you know it's Halloween night and people are sort of crazy - particularly that late at night."

Troy: "That's all right. I'll be okay."

About 2:00 am.

Troy: "Mom, I'm home!"

Next morning:

Troy: "Now I know what you meant about late nights and crazy people."

Mom: "Oh, really?"

Troy: "Yeh, a guy turned left right in front of my car on a really crowded street! And I think he was sort of drunk! That's not a very good place to be that late on Halloween!"

How to ruin the lesson: "I tried to tell you so!"

TIPS TO USE TOMORROW

WHEN TEACHING CHILDREN HOW TO DO NEW THINGS

1. Show them how *and* tell them how.
2. Let them do it. (Risk a little - not too much.)
3. Reinforce, encourage efforts, give specific information about what's right and what needs improvement.
4. Move toward a less directive, more supportive role.
5. Keep kids striving by setting attainable goals while still encouraging them to stretch their abilities.

Decrease in adult direction doesn't mean less direction. It just means the child is doing his or her own directing.

****

HINTS FOR COPING WITH TEENS

—**Actions** speak louder than words!

—Don't waste your energy regretting past mistakes.

—Solve **one** problem at a time.

—Expect improvement - not perfection.

—Children will be unhappy occassionally.

—Never assume a child knows how to do something. **Teach them!**

—Take advantage of outside help when it is needed.

—Have **family fun time - no matter what.** Don't let misbehavior effect it.

MODULE II
PADDLE YOUR OWN CANOE

Shift **responsibility** by refusing to take it!

****

With Rights Come Responsibilities.

TEACHING RESPONSIBILITY:

1. Give kids **responsibilities**
   (Chores, tasks, decisions to make).

2. If they make a **mistake** - or if **all goes well, allow** them the **opportunity** to **experience the consequences.**

3. Then, be sure to **give the responsiblity** *again,* **right away.**

TO GET KIDS TO ACCEPT PROBLEMS AND WANT TO CHANGE

try:

1. Love.

2. Positive stimulation - **encouragement, celebrating** movement in the right direction.

3. Peer pressure.

4. Willingness to **risk.**

5. Willingness to **try.**

Gem

Kids don't do "extra credit" in someone else's garden!

RIGHTS OF PARENTS AND TEACHERS

Here are some examples of rights other parents and teachers have decided they want.

* The right to privacy.

* The right to be free of fear of violence.

* The right to feel secure about my belongings.

* The right to my own time with my spouse and friends.

* The right to some time of my own.

* The right to be treated with courtesy and respect.

* The right to reasonable peace and quiet.

* The right to feel that everyone is carrying his or her responsibilities and that I am not supporting a freeloader.

* The right to lock my classroom or my house and know that it is secure.

****

ELEMENTS OF "GOOD" SCHOOLS, CLASSROOMS, AND FAMILIES

Trust

Sharing

Low level of **excitement**

ELEMENTS OF EFFECTIVE PARENTING

1. Mutual trust

2. Mutual caring and respect

3. Listening

4. Emphasis on assets

5. Open feedback

6. Mutual commitment to common goals and freedom to pursue personal goals

7. Acceptance of imperfect people

Gem

If you have a teen who never makes mistakes, you have a measure of the courage of that teen!

WHOSE PROBLEM WORKSHEET

Teens Problem Pile	My Problem Pile	Our Problem Pile
All things that do not affect my life now or in the future.	All things that affect me personally.	The problem is really the teen's but I am the responsible person.

ACTIVITY ASSIGNMENT

After you get home, take out the list of "Problems" you divided into your Teen's Pile, Your Pile, and Our Pile. Throughout the week, add anything you see yourself doing that should belong on the Kid's Pile.

Watch for an example of when you left a problem with its rightful owner. What happened? How did you feel as you "did not take on the problem"? Make some notes in the space below to share at the next session.

READING ASSIGNMENT

HANDBOOK pp. 27-31

"Communication: A Key to Relationships"
"Using 'I' Messages Effectively"
"Developing Strong Intrapersonal Skills" by Stephen Glenn

Bonus Reading

HANDBOOK pp. 31-44

"Risk the Real World and Common Sense"
"Model Taking Care of Yourself"
"Summary of Talks with Teens About Responsibility"
"Grandma's Rule"
"Adolescent Daydreaming"

Tips to Use Tomorrow

HANDBOOK pp. 45-46

"Alternatives to NO!"
"Cooperation and Household Chores"

COMMUNICATION: A KEY TO RELATIONSHIPS

When most people hear the word **communication**, they think of actions of talking or writing. These actions are taken to initiate or respond to something. Actually, communication is a two-way affair. It involves two major activities:

1. Responding or initiating

2. Listening

However, far more important than our ability to respond or initiate conversations is our ability to **listen.** Hearing and trying to understand messages sent by others are key to developing satisfying relationships.

In our dealings with teens, how we say things greatly affects the outcome. When we have something to express, the words, intonation, and body language chosen to "get the point across" make a difference.

"Clean your room!"

vs.

"I would like your room cleaned before you eat next."

****

"Why can't you ever do it right!"

vs.

"What did you think I asked you to do?"

****

Looking at the floor - "I'm sure glad you were chosen to be a cheerleader."

vs.

A hug, a look straight into the eyes -"I'm sure glad you were chosen to be a cheerleader!"

Since one of people's basic needs is to be **listened to** and **understood,** feelings of being **valued** and **important** are shared when listening is well done.

I'm still trying, but I'm doing lousy in school.

Maybe you should eat a better breakfast or get more sleep or do more homework . . .

You never understand, do you? When a person complains, she doesn't want a solution, she wants sympathy!

-Adapted from Charles Schultz' "Peanuts".

As we listen, it's easy to form our own opinions and think about what we're going to say next. It's difficult but important to thoughtfully listen to the intonation, feelings, and words and to pay attention to facial expresssions and gestures.

It's also important to know when it's appropriate to listen and respond and when it's appropriate to communicate our own feelings.

Communication is a two-way affair

We must be able to:

1. Share ideas and feelings.

2. Interpret the feelings and needs of others.

3. Listen to others.

4. Give and receive love.

5. Cooperate, empathize, and negotiate.

USING "I" MESSAGES EFFECTIVELY

The term "I" message originated with parent and family expert, Thomas Gordon. An "I" message is a powerful way to share our "point of viewing" without imposing it on others.

The real essence of the "I" message is: "These are my ideas, *my* feelings, and they come from **my** needs." The "You" message is a statement about my feelings and ideas about **your** problems or what **you** are doing.

"I" messages are a very successful way to say what we need to say, request what we need, and still take others' feelings and thoughts into account. They are amazingly powerful in getting people to want to do what we need them to do.

If you were on the receiving end of this barrage, how would you feel?

"I've told you over and over again to put the lids on the trash cans so the dogs won't get into them! Honestly, I can't believe you can't do a simple thing like that!"

This is an example of a "You" message. Instead of encouraging the teen's cooperation, this adult has opened the door for resistance, rebellion, and disrespect. No dignity is salvaged here for the teen or the frustrated adult.

What if we heard:

"I get frustrated when I ask you so many times to put the lids on the garbage cans and I come out to find the lids off and the garbage all over the place. I get frustrated because I don't like having this mess when it can be avoided."

Some kids might say, "So?" Most kids will "hear" the underlying message and cooperate.

Why do "I" messages work so well?

1. No orders are given. The decision about what to do is left to the "receiver".

2. There is a strong underlying message that the "receiver" is a person who cares about other people and who is capable and willing to resolve the problem when given enough information.

3. "I" messages are delivered without anger or disrespect.

If we believe kids are basically good and can do what we want them to, then we can believe that "I" messages work. In fact, they work with adults, too! Human beings are basically good and people do care about other people.

"I" messages are made up of three parts:

1. A **description** of the behavior that's bothering us: "When I see the family room is a mess,..." or "When .....happens,....."

2. A statement about our **feelings,** as a result of the behavior: ". . .I feel frustrated . . ."

3. A statement about the **consequences** - for me. ".....because I have to clean it up before I can sit down and relax."

EXAMPLES:

"**When** you are late getting home from your date, I **worry because** I don't know if you are hurt or might need my help in some way."

"**When** you have chores to do and I see you watching TV, I **feel angry and used,because** we agreed you would finish your chores before you relaxed."

"I **get upset when** I have to wait 15 or 20 minutes every day for you to come out after football practice **because** I have planned my activities around picking you up on time."

You can vary the format by changing the parts around.

"Because ... I feel.......when........."

Sometimes we might leave out a part.

"I can't hear what you're saying when there's so much noise."

"I worry about the furniture when you two boys are tussling."

These statements are still non-judgmental information about the consequences of someone else's behavior for us.

An "I" message can be positive, too! "I **feel really happy** for you **when** you tell me about getting an "A" on your research paper **because** I can tell you feel your hard work really paid off!'

Teach the "I" message to your children, your spouse, or your class. Then practice together. You will find that problems can be discussed and resolved much more readily.

And, your needs are more likely to be met!

DEVELOPING STRONG INTRAPERSONAL SKILLS Stephen Glenn

These are skills which an individual uses to communicate with himself and which are important in helping a person develop an understanding of self. Without intrapersonal skills, people do not have the ability to understand their own behavior, cope with the circumstances of life, or control situations in which they find themselves.

These skills cover a wide range of abilities but have the common thread of **self-control.** Examples: the ability to recognize and understand one's own feelings, self-discipline, accepting responsibility, self-control and self-assessment. These skills, and others like them, are critical to an individual if he or she is ever going to set rational goals and meet them. They are also prerequisite for an individual to develop an internal "locus of control".

A "locus of control" is the source an individual uses to define what behavior is appropriate to a given situation and then to provide the impetus to behave in that way. A person without an internal locus of control has to look outside of himself for behavioral cues. Unfortunately, such a person tends to adopt the behaviors of those around him, rather than behave according to the set of values or standards in which he believes.

The lack of intrapersonal skills, then, often leaves one at the mercy of the peer group for many important areas of emotional and social development. Such a person's notion of right or wrong varies depending upon where he is or who is with him. Weaknesses in this area manifest themselves as inability to defer gratification, undeveloped, or underdeveloped self-concept and low self-esteem.

RISK, THE REAL WORLD AND COMMON SENSE

Drugs, sex, alcohol, and cars top the list of most of our worries about teenagers. Because of the potential consequences of teens "pushing" the risks in these four areas, we have a tendency to become even more concerned than the "real world" statistics warrant. On the other hand, it would not make sense to "bury our heads in the sand" and ignore the risks involved with teen exploration of those things. There are those teens who do go beyond the "exploration" stage and others who "get caught" even at the early stages of exploration. It may be the first time a teen has ever joined a group to "drag" or "drink and drive" - it does, in rare cases, become an irretrievable mistake - a risk that ends in death, pregnancy, loss of limb, or hospitalization.

The question is: How do we warn kids of the risks without overprotecting them to the point of rebellion and/ or discouragement?

Adult over-protection begins early. Remember the walks to the city park or the school playground when your three or four-year-old headed straight for a climb on the jungle gym or the bars?

"Don't - you might fall."

"Be careful - you can get hurt"

I had a rule that stood my children and me in good stead during those times -

"Where a child can get up, a child can get down."

I never lifted them onto things - and I let them climb whatever they thought they could manage. When I thought they were really "pushing it", I might say something like, "That looks pretty high - what do you think?" We had a few scraped knees and tumbles. But, we didn't develop the battle which starts, "I'm going to do it! Just because you told me not to!"

Kids don't like the feeling of being hurt. As a result, most of them will take care of themselves if they learn early how to judge and make decisions about doing things that will hurt them. Survival is, after all, a basic law of nature.

As protectors of our teens in potentially "life threatening" situations, we tend to crack down.

We set curfews (as though it's only after midnight that girls get pregnant!).

We ground for breaking rules.

We require parent signatures on everything from grade slips to a day out of school.

We insist on knowing where they are and what they're doing every minute.

I believe we are pushed into these kinds of reactions by real concerns. A percentage of kids who do risk their lives lose them. We must remember it's a very small percentage.

For kids who daily risk their lives with drugs, sex, alcohol, and cars, it's imperative to seek professional help! Even then, we may not be able to help save them.

For the majority of kids, knowledge and information is the best protection we can give if:

1. It is given as we would give it to a neighbor or a friend without undue fear or unrelenting nagging, and

2. The teen believes that hurt from such risks will not pay off in getting back at Mom, Dad, or teachers.

Several examples come to mind:

Jennifer is eight. Her family has moved to a home near a gravel pit that freezes over in the winter. Jennifer is looking forward to ice skating there. Her parents are concerned that she will try to skate when the ice is too thin.

Parent:	"The ice on the gravel pit could be unsafe at times. What do you think would happen if the ice broke and someone fell into the water?"
Jennifer:	"They would get cold and wet."
Parent:	"What else might happen?"
Jennifer:	"Could they get caught under the ice and not be able to get out? That would be scary."
Parent:	"Yes, they could. Do you think a person could get water in his lungs and drown out there?"
Jennifer:	"Uh-huh." (You could see the little wheels going 'round in her head.)

Parent:	"You might want to think about that before you go skating at the gravel pit. We will be happy to go with you the first time to show you how to check the ice to see if it's safe before you go ice-skating."

(The temptation of fearful parents is to go with the child EACH time to check the safety of the ice. The child needs to learn how to "do it herself" and become more capable.)

****

Troy wants to go to a party where he knows there will be liquor.

Dad:	"Troy, you're going to that kegger in Eldorado Springs tonight?"
Troy:	"Yeh."
Dad:	"Many of the kids will be drinking and driving?"
Troy:	"Uh-huh."
Dad:	"You know about the new law that says you lose your license for nine months if you are caught driving while drunk?"
Troy:	"Uh-huh."
Dad:	"I know that we have agreed that you are not going to drink and drive. But sometimes pressure from friends causes kids to change their minds. Any ideas what a kid could say to his friends to stop the pressure?" (Notice the use of "a kid" vs. you?)
Troy:	"Gee, I don't know, Dad."
Dad:	"When I was your age, the guys had one solid rule that we never broke -no matter what."
Troy:	"What was that, Dad?"
Dad:	"It was really simple. The driver did not drink! He *always* stayed sober. Do you think that would work with your friends?"
Troy:	"I think so. Makes good sense to me."
Dad:	"But remember - if, for some reason the driver does have more than he can handle - I will be more than happy to come get you and your friends at anytime, anywhere. Rather do that than go visit the morgue to identify your body."

Sally is 16. Her grades are in bad shape. In fact, she probably won't be able to pull them up to acceptable levels before the end of the semester. This has been a really "low" time for her. She has made a lot of mistakes. She's worried about how some of her friends see her. She knows she can do a lot better than she is doing. Her teacher is concerned and wants to help.

Sally is in tears and obviously very upset.

Mom: "Do you suppose we ought to talk about your grades in Math and choices you have at this point? You really look upset."

Sally: "I am. I guess I really do need some help."

Mom: "Let's put down some of the choices you have. Then you can pick out what is best for you to do right now."

Sally: "Well, I guess I could just not do anything and flunk Math. But then, I'd just have to take it again next year or in summer school. If I have to go to summer school, then I won't be able to go with you and Dad on our trip to Washington and Oregon."

Mom: "You're right. You could take Math this summer and you wouldn't be able to go on the trip with us. You could take Math again next year, just as another idea. I'm sure the school will still be there and no doubt they'll be offering Math again."

Sally: "I wonder if Mr. C. would let me do some extra credit work to bring my grade up. But, with my job I really don't have time to do that. I think it's too late for that anyway. If only I didn't have three finals on one day. I could sure use another night to study!"

Mom: "Well, what do you think of this idea? You could take two of the three finals - probably the two you are most prepared for - and then decide to take the third one the next day. That would give you the extra night you need to study. You would need to go in to your teacher and arrange to make up that final. What do you suppose you could tell him?"

Sally: "That I was sick? Or that I was really too upset to take the test? I suppose I should really say I'm unprepared and I could do a lot better if I had an extra night to study?'

The key in all these examples is open communication with the decision being left to the child.

Occasionally adults get that sixth sense which tells them their teen is looking for a "No" answer or some kind of limit. Young people need the security of knowing that caring adults can sense when they are out of control and unable, for the time being, to make good decisions. At these times they need to know adults will help them by setting limits. There are instances of adult judgement, for which there are no rules, just good common sense and the thought that most decisions turn out all right when the dignity of all remains intact!

MODEL TAKING RESPONSIBILITY FOR YOURSELF

Some parents see their kids failing or in trouble or having a problem and think,

"What can *I* do?"

Or, "What can *we* do?"

Or, "I've done ---."

"I don't understand why my kid doesn't appreciate ---."

Or, ...wants to hurt me like that."

The verbal message is I've done so much for you. The underlying message is: "I put taking care of you first."

A much better strategy is to model taking responsibility for our own well being. Consider these messages: "I love you all very much and I won't do anything to hurt you. So when you are behaving obnoxiously around me, I won't get all out of shape. I will just take care of myself which means, 'Off to your room,' 'Outside.' 'Only you are good company for you right now."

Kids model what their parents do. They learn to take responsibility themselves by example. Then, when they are out driving too fast or too recklessly in a car, their thought wontt be "Won't Dad be mad!" It will be, "I could get hurt by doing this!" They will think less of hurting their parents by getting drunk and more of the consequences to themselves. Failing school becomes a concern for the future rather than a way to "get" parents.

SUMMARY OF TALKS WITH TEENS ABOUT RESPONSIBILITY

As I did the research necessary to write this program, **You've Got To Be Kidding,** I felt it was important that teens share some of their thoughts. I interviewed about 300 teenagers from high schools in the inner city, in the suburbs, and in university settings. I thought their responses to my questions would be different since the culture of the schools was different. I found that teens tend to have similar feelings and thoughts no matter where they go to school.

Question: How do you learn to be responsible?

Replies: "Let us make a lot of our own decisions - and then when we make them - don't judge them."

"Let us discover the consequences."

EXAMPLE:

Parent: "It's your money!"

The teen goes out and buys a shirt that he or she likes.

Parent: "You spent all your money on **that!**"

Teens say the message is: "It's really not *my* money."

"Give us jobs to do - and then don't bug us - we'll get them done! If you have to have them done by a certain time - tell us the time and then let *us* schedule it in."

"Let us know when we've done a good job - not just when we've done a poor one."

"Let us know you really believe we can do it."

"Spoiling can make us lazy. Give us responsibilities early so we can learn how to handle it."

Question: Do you think there ought to be consequences for not being responsible?

Replies: "Sure - but if you only make a little mistake, once - I don't think they ought to climb all over your case."

"Sometimes - I just don't want to do it right then, and then I forget. It isn't that I really meant to. So I guess I'd like to be reminded, but probably just once. Then my Mom can get mad."

"My Mom puts 'nice notes' on my bed when I do a good job cleaning up my room, or if I go some place I'll find an 'I love you' note in my sleeping bag."

"I think the consequences ought to be fair. My brother gets away with a lot of stuff that I don't 'cause he's a boy!"

"Teachers ought to be consistent. If we're supposed to be in class on time, they ought to get there on time, too. If there's an excuse for them, there's one for us, too!"

Question: Do you want your parents and teachers to help you?

Replies: "When they know I'm in trouble or when I ask for it."

"Sometimes it seems like teachers want you to fail - like it's some kind of a contest -and if you do bad, they win."

"Sometimes it's hard to get them to listen to me."

"I'd rather ask my friends about my problems. Adults just don't understand."

"I wish I had some adult I could talk with about my problems who would understand."

"Jim's Dad is super. He remembers what it's like to be a kid. He tells us about mistakes he made. He has time to talk to us. I love to go over to his house!"

"I wish my Mom would spend more time talking to me."

"I wish they would ask my opinion some of the time."

Question: Tell me about the best teacher you ever had.

Replies: "My music teacher", "The coach", "Miss ...." (In any given school, most kids picked the same two or three teachers.)

"I can't think of any."

Question: Why did you pick (the music teacher, the coach, Miss ......)?

Replies: "S/he cares about whether I learn or not."

"S/he listens to me and treats me like a real person."

"S/he knows when I need help."

"S/he makes me work hard and I learn a lot."

"S/he made me believe I could do things when I didn't think I could."

GRANDMA'S RULE

Grandma's Rule: First You Work, Then You Play!

"You may leave for school *after* you've taken the garbage out!"

"You may go to the meeting *after* you've fed the dogs."

"You may use the phone *after* the homework is done."

To which most teens will say, "But I'll be late!" or "I don't have time!" or "But I need to talk to Sue."

Getting up, eating, gathering books, lunch money, homework, getting to the bus on time, getting to classes with paper, pencil and books, doing chores are all kids' jobs. It is important that kids do their jobs themselves. They need to deal with the natural consequences of disorganization, sleeping late, and goofing off. Adults worry that kids will go hungry, miss a good time, do poorly in school, and hurt when the consequences fall. So they rescue, direct and supervise, keep track of time, remember, and generally hassle their heads over kids who aren't getting things done.

Kids will tell you they are really busy, and lots of them are! However, remember when you had lots of things happening at once, and you surprised yourself by getting them all done - and done well! When I hit that point, I know I have to take stock of my priorities - the "have to's" and the "put off until tomorrows". Teens can, too! And they'll know they can if they have a chance to practice.

The real world requires: First you work. Then you get paid. Then you eat! Best we teach this survival principle to our children as early as possible. In our house it is called "Grandma's Rule"!

What if you've done "kid's jobs" for your teens. What if you've done lots of reminding and directing on those they've done themselves, and you decide to change? How is this change best accomplished?

First - let your teen know you plan to change and how - calmly, matter-of-factly, and with confidence.

DIALOG EXAMPLES:

Mom: "The school attendance office called today to say you are not going to classes regularly. As you know, they have called me about this problem in the past."

Tonya: "Yeh."

Mom: "Usually, when the school calls about your skipping classes, I get upset. I make myself even more upset when I try to think of a consequence that will make you want to go to school. Then I get really frustrated when I realize nothing that I do can really **make you** go to school."

Tonya: "So?"

Mom: "Well, I've decided that your going to school is not my problem. When I had a chance to go to school, I had to decide what I was going to do. Now, it's your turn."

Tonya: "Really?"

Mom: "Yes. It's even possible you might decide not to go to school any more."

Tonya: "Really!"

Mom: "It's possible. If you decide to go to school, I will know that you are still preparing yourself for getting a job and living on your own resources. I will help you all I can. When you decide you're finished with school, I will know you've decided that you're prepared for getting a job and living on your own. If you continue living here, room and board payments begin. If you choose to live somewhere else, I will wish you good luck and enjoy visiting you when I'm asked. I know you will make a good decision."

Dad: "John, each morning I wake you when I come down to turn on the coffee. Then, I awaken you again after my shower. Mom wakes you a third time when she comes down to fix breakfast. We find that we become upset and feel anxious about whether you're going to get up in time to dress, eat, and catch the bus. We bought you this alarm clock so you can get yourself up in the morning. Mom and I will be happy to have you join us for breakfast, if you decide you have time."

****

Teacher: "Class, I find that I give assignments a couple of weeks ahead of time and remind you several times before they're actually due. I asked myself - why do I do this? I think I'm telling you it's OK to forget; I will remind you. I don't think I like giving you that message so I am going to make up assignments on a weekly basis. I will hand out an assignment sheet each Tuesday. It will be up to you to make a note of when things are due and turn them in then. I suspect you will feel better knowing I believe you can handle that responsibility. I know I will."

Next, (and the hardest part), **mean it!** Stick to your guns in the face of "You didn't ---" and "It's not fair!" and "You always ---" and "I'll be late!" "I'll miss my bus." "You don't want me to fail, do you?" If you think you are about to give in, take a break from the conversation, pleading, and accusations and go to the bathroom!

Rudolph Dreikurs acquainted me with this "Go to the Bathroom" idea years ago when I read his book, *Children: The Challenge*. It has worked for me many times. The bathroom is the one place kids don't follow us. We have a chance to rethink and regroup.

Given a number of opportunities to discover we are no longer responsible for their jobs, teens will begin to realize we mean what we say and are doing what we said we'd do! When you can say with love, "Honey, I know it's hard to learn these things *and* I know you can take care of it." Kids will test your resolve and soon take on these responsibilities for themselves.

Some hints for handling procrastinations:

1. Make lists of jobs to be done. Check them off when they're done.

2. Set time limits - many of us work on things at the last minute. If we know there is a back end to when things have to be done, we'll make it.

3. Do it, instead of waiting for teens to do it, with the understanding that time lost now will be made up later.

EXAMPLE:

When Jay comes home from school, he finds a note on the kitchen table.

> Dear Jay,
>
> Hope you enjoyed your Olympics-of-the-Mind today at school.
>
> I would appreciate coming home to a family room and kitchen that are cleaner than the ones I left this morning.
>
> Love,
> Mom

Mom gets home about 5:30 p.m. The note is gone and the rooms look the same. So, before dinner preparation begins, out comes the dust rag and vacuum.

Jay: "Mom, the Science Fair is tonight at school."

Mom: "Oh? What time?"

Jay: "7:00. Can we go?"

Mom: "Well, let's see. I need to finish cleaning the family room and kitchen. Then get dinner. Then, I want to relax a bit and read the paper. Hum-m-m. I don't think I'll make it."

Jay: (Hopefully) "Will you make it with some help?"

Mom: "I might!"

4. Find someone who wants to do the job and collect the "payoff".

EXAMPLE:

The lawn needs to be mowed. Volunteer gets ticket money and a ride to the movies.

5. Make a Sunday collection box. Pick up those things that "bug" you. Store them in a box for reclaim on Sunday.

6. Leave a "note".

EXAMPLES:

On the mirror:

> HELP! HAIRS IN MY DRAIN LEAVE ME
> CLOGGED! Ugh!
> THANKS. YOUR CLEANED UP SINK.

From the plant:

> WATER ME, PLEASE!

From the dirty dishes in the family room:

> HELP! THE BUGS ARE GETTING ME!
> YOUR SNACK DISHES.

My son, Scott, made a deal with his Dad to keep one side of the garage clean if he could build and store his boat on the other side. The boat building had crept over to the "clean" side once too often and I heard my husband declare, under his breath, the boat had to go!

Note on the garage door:

> Dear Scott,
>
> I am such a mess Dad is threatening to take away my friend, BOAT. HELP!
>
> Signed,
> Lonely Garage

When I got home that night I found a clean garage and this note on the door.

```
Dear Garage,

        I do hope you can keep friend,
BOAT, now!.

             Signed,
             Scott
```

Humor and the adult belief that kids really do have good intentions help develop a cooperative atmosphere.

7. Use assertive messages.

EXAMPLES:

Bobby: "Mom, I don't have time!"

Mom: "I understand you want to do it later AND (better than BUT) I want the kitchen cleaned up so I can cook dinner."

****

Jamie: "Miss Jones, I just couldn't get my homework done last night."

M.Jones: "I appreciate how busy you are *and* the assignment is due by the end of the school day."

****

John: "That's not fair!"

Mom: "You're wondering why Jane doesn't have to do more of the work **and I'd like the yard raked.**"

John: "But Jane hardly does anything!"

Mom: "I guess you think Jane gets away with a lot **and** I'd like the yard raked."

John: "But Mom, I know, you'd like the yard raked. OK, but Jane gets to help!"

This technique is sometimes called the "broken record".

ADOLESCENT DAYDREAMING

Scott spent the first month and a half of last summer's vacation looking for a job - sort of. I really didn't see the effort put forth that I "knew" was required to land a job. The rest of the time he spent mixed between an activity or two with his friends and reclining on his bed, his radio blaring -reading or just lying there with his hands behind his head, staring at the ceiling. While I watched his summer slipping away and tried not to say much, he just "wasted away" his time.

I worried that he wouldn't get a job in time to earn the money he wanted to save for buying a car when he turned 16. I worried that he was feeling really discouraged because his job hunting efforts weren't working very well. I worried that maybe his Dad and I ought to be helping him more than we were to get that job. I worried that this would just be an awful summer for him to remember -boring, not productive, nothing to do, no money, etc.!

Halfway through the summer he got a job. And the summer - as I saw it - got progressively better from there.

On the way home from football practice this fall, Scott and I were talking about the summer and he said, "I had one of the best summers I've ever had!"

You can imagine my surprise!!

So I said,

"That really surprises me. I thought it must have been awful because you had so little to do at the beginning of the summer. All you seemed to do was lay around a lot."

"Yeh, Mom. That's what was great about it! I had time to just lay around. I read a lot - just for fun - not the stuff I have to read for school. And I had lots of time to think."

"What did you think about?"

"Oh, lots of things. Like what do I want to do after I graduate from high school. I think about what it would be like to be in the Army, or be a computer expert, or a doctor, or work on construction - you know. I think about what kinds of cars I could buy and what I might like and dislike about each one."

I have heard many adults complain about the time kids just waste -the hours on the phone with friends - the hours spent just lying around.

While it is very true that kids must learn that things don't just happen without effort, it is also important that they develop the habit of giving themselves "thinking time".

Our society has dealt with the pressures created through "work-a-holism" by courses in stress reduction, health foods, exercises, jogging, meditation, yoga, and a host of other activities designed to give our bodies rest and time for "day dreaming".

Teens do this naturally! - given the opportunity. It is productive time for trying on various life roles, working out alternative solutions to problems, and space to just let their minds wonder - to dream. It is a time for trying out and collecting ideas and reactions from their friends.

Remember when as girls we tried to picture our "knight in shining armor" in our mind's eye? Or as boys, we "saw" ourselves as tremendously successful - or a real stud? It is particularly interesting that psychologists say: "The probability of becoming something is directly related to being able to envision ourselves as that something in our imagination - in our mind's eye."

A fat person will only become thin if she/ he can imagine themselves as thin. We can only be successful as teachers and parents if we can "see" ourselves successful in our mind's eye.

So don't be mislead by the hours of what appears to be pointless conversations and lying around. This time can be a very meaningful part of growing for our children. We encourage creative imaginings and "play" with younger children. We expect "work" from adults. Our teens are in the middle!

TIPS TO USE TOMORROW

ALTERNATIVES TO "NO"

One of my pet peeves is kids who hit me with requests to do things or "Mom, will you ----?" as I walk in the door. My arms are loaded down with my briefcase, the mail, a bag of groceries, the newspaper -- and the dog is jumping on my stockings to be petted. My reflex reaction at that moment is, "No!"

Here are some suggestions given by Barbara Coloroso as part of her material called *Winning at Teaching without Beating Your Kids.* Since hearing these ideas, I haven't had to say "no" nearly so often - nor do I get 'hit' with the barrage of questions I used to get as I walked in the door.

1. *"Give me a minute to think about it."* Now my kids say to me --"I'll give you a minute to think about it," or "Can you take a minute to think about ------?"

2. *"Convince me."* My teens have learned to build a convincing case with facts and complete information before they ask. The flip side is that I must be reasonable in my response.

3. *"Yes -- with conditions."* It is harder to argue with a "yes", even when there are requirements such as "work before play" or "dinner before dessert".

EXAMPLE:

"Yes, after dinner you can have a cookie."

"No" as a Control

A few thoughts:

1. I will use "no" as rarely as possible.

2. When I do say "no", I will mean it.

COOPERATION AND HOUSEHOLD CHORES

"Chores" keep the family or classroom running smoothly. Usually, participation in keeping the family going is a child's first adventure in group living. It is in this setting he or she first becomes aware of **being genuinely needed.**

Meet as a family and

—List all jobs necessary to keep the family going smoothly.

—Decide what results are desired and when each chore is to be done. To "do it *my* way (the kid's way) is OK." It's the results that count.

—Make up a schedule.

—Vary who does what for **variety**.

When the family does this together, each member feels important.

Routine, according to Dreikurs, "is to a child what walls are to a house". It gives boundaries and dimensions, security, consistency, and structure. (That's why summer often drives us crazy!) However, because of the many demands on their time, it is awfully hard to get teens to stay with a routine. So make routines flexible when priorities require a change.

Kids and adults usually agree there should be consequences for chores forgotten or not done because this creates problems for others. Meeting with the family helps here, too, since kids are more likely to stick to the rules they've helped make.

Incentives That Have Worked For Others:
1. Job exchange between kids and parents.

2. Favorite meals on nights particular kids have chores.

3. Note reminders.

4. When checking for quality ask: "Would I hire you back next week to do the same job?" Kids will usually answer pretty honestly.

Remember: As teachers and parents, it's important that kids do as we ask. **It's OK for them not to like it.** If we ask them to go to their room, and they "lip off" on the way out, it's OK. We don't like paying our taxes, but we do it, and we "lip off" while doing it.

MODULE III
COMMUNICATION AND DIALOG

Gem

Solve your problem any way you like,
Just don't make it a problem for anyone else.

—Jim Fay

The A-B-C of Rational Adjustment

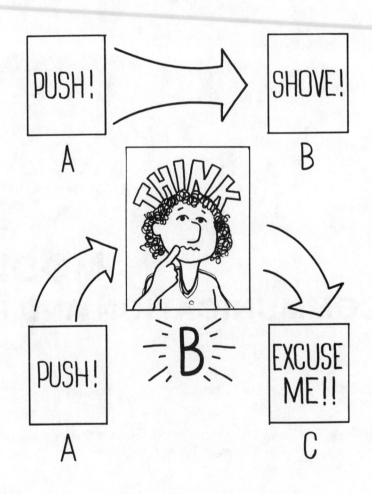

RESPONSIBILITY - WHAT MAKES IT SO HARD TO GIVE?

Here are some commonly held beliefs which make it hard to give responsibility to teens:

1. I am trying to be a **good** parent or teacher. Being a **good** parent or teacher means: (Write some of the things **good** parents or teachers should do in the space below.)

2. It's my job to guide my child. It's his or her job to follow my direction.

3. I'm supposed to be able to teach every child. It is my job to see to it that all learn and are successful in school. (Are learning and successful the same things?)

4. I'm obligated to care for my child. He or she didn't ask to be born!

5. If my student falls behind in school, it's my job to see to it that he or she gets the help he or she needs.

6. It's my job to be alert to dangerous situations and protect my children (students) from them.

7. It's my job to protect my child from suffering.

8. My child's happiness is worth any sacrifice I might make.

9. I can make my kids behave.

10. In my house (classroom) I'm the chief and the kids are the tribe.

11. Teens shouldn't be bored. I am responsible for keeping them busy. It keeps them off the streets!

12. My kids won't love me if ....
(Finish this sentence.)

13. If I just did a better job, my teen would do well in school, would behave better, etc.

14. I am responsible for the behavior of my class.

15. List others in the space below.

BLOCKS TO COMMUNICATION

1. Failure to separate **fact** from **opinion.**

2. Failure to consider the **levels** of Communication.

    a. **Words**

    b. **Body Language**

TRANSLATING "YOU" MESSAGES INTO "I" MESSAGES

1. "Joe, must you continue to make that racket. I've told you five times that you are disturbing me. Now you're making me angry!"

2. "Eric, sit down and do your homework. The rest of the class is being disturbed by your roaming around."

3. "Your constant complaining is really getting to me!"

4. "Hey, that's not fair! Why do I always have to do the dirty jobs?"

5. "You make me so nervous I could scream!"

6. "You administrators are always telling us that every student can learn! What do you think I am, Superwoman (man)?"

7. "What do you mean, I always take advantage of you?"

8. "You didn't even consider my feelings when you decided to buy that!"

9. "If you don't quit shouting at me, I'm going to send you to the Principal!"

10. "Don't talk to me like that!"

MEANING, PURPOSE, and **SIGNIFICANCE** in **Life** come from being:

Listened to

Taken seriously

Genuinely needed

What if:

1. People didn't listen to us?

2. We didn't feel needed by someone?

3. No one took us seriously?

How do teens feel?

DIALOG helps us determine what has Meaning, Purpose, and Significance in our Lives and the lives of others. Through Dialog, we can find the answers to these important questions:

1. **What** happened?

2. **Why** is it important or significant?

3. **How** is it important in the future?

****

FEELING WORDS

Try to think of additional feeling words that have slightly different or about the same meaning.

Happy	pleased	excited	thrilled
Angry	_____	_____	_____
Stupid	_____	_____	_____
Lonely	_____	_____	_____
Discouraged	_____	_____	_____
Proud	_____	_____	_____
Glad	_____	_____	_____
Resentful	_____	_____	_____
Afraid	_____	_____	_____
Nervous	_____	_____	_____
Frustration	_____	_____	_____

You will find more **feeling words** in Tips to Use Tomorrow on pp. 68-69

ACTIVITY ASSIGNMENT

Describe a situation in your classroom or at home where you think an "I" message is in order. In the space below, identify how you **feel** about the situation.

Then write down an "I" message you want to try.

Now, **try it.**

What reaction did you get? Be ready to discuss it during the next session.

****

During the week, pick an experience which should have taught your teen something. Take the time to discuss the experience with him or her using the three dialog questions:

What happened? What was significant or important about the experience?

Why or **How** was it significant or important?

How will it affect whatever you think, do, or feel next time or in the future?

Be prepared to share how the discussion went, using the same DIALOG questions.

READING ASSIGNMENT

HANDBOOK pp. 54-59

"Natural and Logical Consequences"
"Logical and Natural Consequences vs. Punishment"
"Three Approaches to Discipline for Parents and Teachers" by Stephen Glenn
"Natural and Logical Consequences: How Do We Know When We've Got One?"
"Teaching Good Judgement" by Stephen Glenn

Bonus Reading

HANDBOOK pp. 60-66

"Three Perceptions" by Stephen Glenn
"Assertiveness: A Skill We all Need"
"Family Meetings" by Stephen Glenn
"Con Games"

Tips to Use Tomorrow

HANDBOOK pp. 66-69

"Dealing with Conflict - Questions to Disarm Disagreements"
"On Telling the Truth"
"Words to Express Feelings"

NATURAL AND LOGICAL CONSEQUENCES

It is very hard for anyone to understand the importance of their behavior if they rarely experience the natural or logical consequences that come of that behavior. In 1930, the child was born into a world in which logical and natural consequences were a daily experience.

If you came home on your horse really fast, and it was all lathered up, and you did not walk it before you put it in the stall, it dropped dead. Then you walked everywhere for a while. It was rather clearly connected.

If you did not go out and split wood and bring it in and stoke up the fire at night, you woke up cold. You went back out in the morning and cut the wood you should have cut the night before. Consequences were clearly associated with things that you did.

They are not today. There is very little connection between our actions and the consequences. Social and environmental changes have eliminated many opportunities for young people to experience consequences. Thus, they are deprived from learning some of life's greatest lessons. While consequences may not be the most pleasant way to learn, for many of us it is the only lasting one.

LOGICAL/NATURAL CONSEQUENCES vs. PUNISHMENT

There are a number of "expert" opinions regarding the use of punishment as a way to get kids to behave differently:

"NEVER use punishment."

"Punishment is OK up to a certain age."

—A traffic ticket could be considered a punisher.

—An "F" on a test could be a punisher.

—Being singled out as a particularly bright student could be a punisher.

The following chart describes the difference between punishment delivered by an adult to a child (often in anger and causing pain) vs. consequences (either natural or logical) delivered in a calm environment, in order to change behavior. While the terms, "punishment" and "consequences", may be interchangeable, in this program we will use the term "consequences" to describe a desirable environment and "punishment" to describe an undesirable environment.

LOGICAL/NATURAL CONSEQUENCES	vs.	PUNISHMENT
TO DO		NOT TO DO

1. Comes from the reality of the social order (REAL WORLD) with the child comparing wishes with actual outcomes.
 	
   1a. Assertive—Tells the other guy where we stand.
	1. Comes from adult imposition of power. Usually painful and based on retribution or revenge.
	
	   1a. Aggressive—Tells the other guy where to go.

2. Concerned with what will happen NOW. Can develop a new plan of reacting or acting.	2. Based on past behavior. Options closed to individual.
3. Comes from within—assumed by the DOER. Internal control.	3. Is imposed—done to someone. Responsibility outside the child's control.
4. Emphasis on teaching ways to act that will result in more successful outcomes and problem solving.	4. Focus on negative attention and power.
5. Friendly—as would occur with a neighbor.	5. Usually delivered with open or concealed anger.
6. Focus on WHAT TO DO—encourage desirable behavior.	6. Tells what NOT TO DO—curbing undesirable.
7. Difficult and time consuming for adults.	7. Easy or expedient for the adults.
8. This is how I am going to take care of myself.	8. This is what I am going to do to you.

Adults usually catch themselves using punishment with kids when they are angry or really don't know what else to do. Also authority, control, and punishment were the approaches used when we were growing up. However, punishment tends to lose its power and effectiveness as kids grow older. Hurt, resentment, and guilt are generated.

We wouldn't think of punishing our friends, neighbors, or spouses (if the relationship is OK). Punishment teaches kids to avoid adults when they make mistakes. Opportunities to guide and influence teens are cut since they, like us, don't want to spend time or request advice from folks who yell, scold, and moralize.

Our goal, as "growers" of children, is to develop youth who feel capable and confident in their abilities to solve problems and control themselves and their world. Kids who experience the consequences of their behavior are given the opportunity to practice solving problems and making decisions. They learn, through their successes and mistakes, that they are capable and in control of their lives.

THREE APPROACHES TO DISCIPLINE FOR PARENTS AND TEACHERS

STEPHEN GLENN

STRICTNESS
(Excessive Control)

1. Based on power or personal authority. Is usually painful and based on retribution or revenge (what happened in the past). Is arbitrary.

2. Is imposed. (Done to someone.) Responsibility is assumed by the punisher.

3. Options for the individual are closed. No chance to improve behavior.

4. A teaching process which usually reinforces failure identity. Essentially negative and short term without sustained personal involvement.

5. Open or concealed anger.

6. Easy or expedient.

7. External locus of control.

8. Breaks involvement.

PRODUCES:

Anger, violence, frustration, hostility.

CORRELATED WITH

Homicide, suicide, alcohol abuse, lack of achievement and productivity, vandalism.

FIRMNESS
(With Dignity and Respect)
Leads to Self-Discipline

1. Based on logical or natural consequences expressing the need for self-control in an organized society. (Rules which must be learned in order to function adequately.) Concerned with what will happen now.

2. Responsibility is assumed by the individual (what they have done to themselves). Comes from within. Is accepted.

3. Options are kept open so individuals can choose to improve behavior.

4. An active teaching process involving close, sustained, personal involvement. Emphasizes teaching ways to act that will result in more successful behavior.

5. Friendly, supportive.

6. Difficult and time consuming.

7. Internal locus of control.

8. Maintains involvement.

PRODUCES:

Security, motivation, wellness.

CORRELATED WITH:

Motivation, achievement, resistance to peer influence, resistance to drug and alcohol abuse, respect for authority and productivity.

PERMISSIVENESS
(Excessive Autonomy)

1. Based on feelings (affect), guilt, and illogical consequences.

2. Responsibility is not clearly defined and often avoided by everyone.

3. Options are often ignored in favor of feelings and promises.

4. Teaching is ignored in favor of emotional gratification, apologies, promises.

5. Ambivalent, insecure, confused.

6. Easy or expedient.

7. No clear locus of control, out of control.

8. Conditional involvement.

PRODUCES:

Lack of motivation, frustration, insecurity.

CORRELATED WITH:

Excess peer influence, high marijuana use, lack of achievement, promiscuity.

NATURAL AND LOGICAL CONSEQUENCES: HOW DO WE KNOW WHEN WE'VE GOT ONE?

Two types of consequences

Natural: when consequences of our social environment fall on the individual without anyone deciding to impose them.

EXAMPLES:

It is a natural consequence when:

We leave too late for the airport;
Get caught in traffic and miss our plane or;
I leave my package in the rest room, discover my mistake, return to get it only to find someone has taken it.

When natural consequences occur, such as a child losing a coat left at the ball game, we can respond with understanding and say:

"Bummer!"
"Too bad that happened! I wonder what you could do differently next time?"
"How might you look for it now?"

Imposed (logical): when the action causes a problem for someone else who then imposes consequences in order to get the person creating the problem to change.

EXAMPLES:

Teachers impose consequences for students who do poor work or who talk incessantly in class.

Parents impose consequences for chores not done, for coming in later than agreed, and for fighting with brothers and sisters.

As an aside, remember there are **positive,** natural, and imposed logical consequences for doing well.

EXAMPLES:

We always feel good when we pass a patrolman on the highway and we know the red light will not be blinking for us because we're within the speed limit.

We can enjoy a night out when we know we are organized and ready for the next day.

Imposed consequences are best approached in one of two ways:

A. Reminder of the agreement. "I'm surprised *you* decided to stay in for the next three evenings instead of coming home at 11:00 tonight as we agreed."

B. "I" statements about my feelings and how I plan to take care of myself. "I am afraid you will break something fighting in the house. Please continue - outside!"

Kids generally know the rules. When they decide to "forget" or not do something, they will often come up with their own "imposed" consequences provided they feel good about their relationship with us. In fact, many kids are too hard on themselves! However, if "I don't know" is the stock response for "What can we do next time?", we need to set external limits which are logical, realistic, and maintain the dignity and respect of all.

So how do we know when we've done that?

1. Does it help the teen learn what to do in the future in a similar situation?

2. Is the consequence similar to what would happen to an adult who acted that way in the real world? Is it relevant in time and place?

3. Will this consequence help the teen feel more capable of solving his or her own problems?

4. Does the consequence maintain the teen's dignity and self-respect?

5. Will the teen believe that s/he is the cause of the discomfort or will s/he blame adults for the "punishment"?

We need to keep in mind that our role is to **guide** (not force) and **influence** - to be available for advice while allowing kids to learn from their mistakes. Also, keep in mind, people don't learn as well when they're angry or scared!

TEACHING GOOD JUDGMENT   Stephen Glenn

Good judgment is a product of experience - but it is more than that. We know this because we all have experience, but we don't all have good judgment. The development of judgment comes when we understand our experiences.

What has happened?
Why did that happen?
What could we do next time so that it might not happen again (or so that it will happen again, if the experience was positive)?

In order to make a judgment we must be able to determine:

1. What is significant about the experience?
2. Why is that significant?
3. How does it affect the decisions I make in the future? How does it or will it affect my actions in the future?

As children learn to apply these questions, they will understand themselves and their experiences well enough to make good judgments.

THREE PERCEPTIONS Stephen Glenn

You have a list of the Significant Seven on pp. 5-6 in Module I of your **HANDBOOK.** Included in the following article are three perceptions about ourselves that allow us to think of ourselves as capable.

1. I am **capable** - learned through identification with viable role models.

As strong, capable individuals we have people around us who we want to be like—(heroes). These are people whose life patterns are viable - they are productive, self-sufficient, and reasonably happy people.

Children learn to be what they have seen and experienced. What they are told is far less significant than what they see. It only follows that they need capable role models. Not only do role models need to be available, young people need to be able to identify with them. They must want to be like the models and see themselves as able to be like them. If an individual can visualize himself as being like a strong or viable person in his environment, then he has a goal which can be reached. This goal begins to shape behavior and help him make both small and large decisions.

The high-risk person, on the other hand, has not learned to see himself as a capable person. Therefore, he does not identify with or behave like people who are dealing capably with the same kinds of situations in which he finds himself. When problems arise, he depends on someone else to explain to him what happened, why it happened, and what he should do about it. This fosters dependency. He does not know how to survive. When he gets stuck, he does not know why he is stuck. He has the same experience over and over again without learning from it and without gaining an awareness of how others succeed.

A teacher stated that every year she likes to give a writing assignment that goes like this: List your ten favorite adult heroes and tell what makes them admirable. Ten years ago, it was a 30-minute in-class assignment. The kids wrote about the astronauts, their parents, their pastor, the president. "Five years ago, I had to make it a take-home job so they could think it over, because offhand, they couldn't think of anyone. Last year, I reduced the list to five people and gave them three days to complete it, and still one or two said ruefully, 'There's no one.'"

2. I **contribute in meaningful ways** and I'm **genuinely needed** - learned through identification with and responsibility for "family" processes.

I would suggest three ways to help parents become effective role models for children.

Always Treat a Child As If He Is Capable. Parents can assist children in determining a positive view of themselves by treating them as if they were capable. Children will view themselves in the way they think others see them. When children hear others call them "shy" or "clumsy," they tend to think of themselves as shy or clumsy. When people use phrases such as, "Why can't you ever?" children think they never do anything right.

Parents can sustain a child's feelings of capability when giving correction. Our conversations should be more like, "You did a naughty thing. This surprises me, because you are such a good girl."

Always remember, **A Child is Not Just a Short Adult.** A child has a different perspective on the world, sees things in different time frames, has different conceptual abilities, and is in the middle of developmental tasks that are different from those of an adult.

When adults forget this important point, they fall into a trap which undermines the child's self-concept. This trap is what we call "adultisms." An adultism is treating a young person as though he should view life through the values and perspective that an adult uses. To expect the children to have an adult perspective leads to feelings of powerlessness and inferiority as they feel they do not measure up to these adult perceptions and expectations.

Some may want to defend their use of the adult perspective, saying, "After all, aren't we as adults right? Don't we have more wisdom and experience? Don't we have the responsibility to teach, guide, and protect?" Absolutely. So let's go at it in an effective way.

In order for a child to develop into a capable adult he must see himself as contributing in a meaningful way to things greater than himself. A child must feel his life matters and that he is significant and needed. Recent studies into cults show that they feed on those who are not taken seriously nor listened to; those who feel no one needs them. Learning to take our children seriously and listening to them allows them to develop feelings that they are contributing and are genuinely needed. When this need is not met, the child is vulnerable to individuals or groups which make him feel important.

Beyond cults, however, there is a greater potential that this youngster will gradually slip into undesirable behavior or adopt values of his peer group where he does feel important or needed.

This problem is of fairly recent origin. Children in the rural environment had substantial interaction time with parents and made significant contributions to the family's livelihood. Today, with modern conveniences and our rapid pace of life, children have few ready-made opportunities to significantly contribute to others around them.

Contributions Must be Genuinely Needed

Before a child can effectively contribute to others, he must feel that what he is contributing is significant. In any project in which the child is involved, it should be the learning or the improvement that is the focus, rather than the appearance of the final product. Leaders who give constructive criticism and let the child continue in his progress will allow the child to see himself as capable of contributing significantly. The child will develop the attitude that what he does "matters" to others.

A child will see himself as he perceives others see him. Adults who foster the child's seeing himself as significant prevent feelings of uselessness in the child.

3. I can **influence** what happens to me through my faith in personal resources to solve problems.

This skill refers to the ability and attitudes necessary to work through problems and the belief that they can be solved through application of personal resources. When these skills are poorly developed, a person believes that problems have been escaped if he can't feel them any more. (The escape is often accomplished through the use of alcohol or drugs.) He believes that there is nothing he can do about the present or the future; things just happen to him.

The dependent person has not learned, or does not believe, that he has resources within himself to deal with problems. He does not believe his life is shaped to a large degree by what he decides and does. Instead, he believes that solutions to problems are faith, luck, and other things outside himself. Things either happen or they do not happen.

To a great extent, this learning is a product of our leisure lifestyle, the media, and contemporary family patterns. Because we have leisure time and disposable income, fewer of our children have any significant experience in doing without. From an early age, we are able to fulfill a very impressive array of wants, not to mention needs. The lack of a consistent experience in doing without leads people to believe that it is an abnormal deprivation, rather than a very real part of life for all of us. Because of this, there is no understanding of where things come from or the effort required to obtain them. They arrive miraculously.

The problem is compounded by family patterns which no longer teach the individual the relationship between work and obtaining a livelihood. When the family effort was centered on the farm or in a small town, occupations and income were on display. Bad times were not uncommon and they were discussed. Today's family patterns, with electronic deposit of funds earned far from home and payment by check and credit card, do not lend themselves to teaching children the basic economic facts of life.

Perhaps one of the great teachers that problems are solved miraculously is the media. The most prevalent is, of course, television. In both programming and advertising, miracle resolutions to problems are demonstrated over and over.

Superman, Wonder Woman, and Charlie's Angels always show up just in the nick of time. Don't the bad guys miss when they shoot, while the hero is an unerring marksman? Problems are solved *for* us and not *by* us.

As a child experiences opportunities to affect what happens to him, he begins to see himself as having power. This allows him to develop the perception that his life is not controlled entirely by fate, luck, or people outside himself.

The child who feels capable knows that he can change his feelings or actions and, therefore, affect the ways in which he is treated. He recognizes the value of his own contribution to those close to him and how such contributions influence what happens to him in return. He knows that what he does makes a difference. If he studies over and over, he gets a good grade and then is helped to see how the study influences his grade.

The capable child is said to have a sense of **internal control.** He learns that life is often what he makes it and not always something that happens to him by luck or fate.

Helplessness

A child is said to have external control when a parent fails to connect what the child does with what he gets. That is, he looks to others, for magic or instant solutions to make the difference in life. He sees himself as powerless and a victim of life's tumultous passages. He hopes for good luck and accepts the bad as inevitable. Whenever parents react to situations by controlling the outcome, children may feel powerless and incapable.

It is difficult for a child to believe in cause and effect when a promised event doesn't happen or when what should happen doesn't (illogical consequences). Life can sometimes be very illogical. Parents, however, who minimize the frequency of illogical consequences can help develop the idea that what I do matters, that I can make a difference.

Help young people understand what happens to them in their lives and how they can gain control over what happens. Explore situations so the young person will come to an understanding of what occurs in his life, and do it in a way that he sees himself as capable.

Whenever a parent tells a child, "This is what happened, and this is what you should do," he is really saying, "Listen, dummy, quit trying to think for yourself. If you had just left the thinking up to me, everything would have been all right." The parent reinforces the child in incapabilities rather than capabilities. A more helpful message would be, "What happened?" "What caused it to happen?" "How could you do it next time?"

ASSERTIVENESS

Assertiveness is the behavior pattern we need in order to model effective **taking care of ourselves.** Assertiveness is:

1. The ability to express honest thoughts and feelings to others.
2. The ability to ask for and get our rights and,
3. The ability to do this (1) and (2) while taking into account the thoughts and feelings of others.

If we are not in the habit of taking care of ourselves by stating our needs and expecting that they will be met, change is hard. It will take practice.

Some thoughts and beliefs that make it hard to take care of ourself:

1. People won't like me!
   Learn to be assertive.
   Make up an assertive statement that fits.
   Try your statement in front of your mirror.
   Listen to it as you say it.
   Guess someone's response to your statement.
   Try a few "wishes" out in fairly *safe* places.
   See what happens.
2. People will get angry with me!

   Use the same practice as in #1.
   Try it!

3. I'll hurt others' feelings.

   Check this belief out with people who will be honest with you *and* care about you. "How badly would you feel if I said ...?"
   You may get information that will help you change what you say so it works well for you.

4. I'll be ignoring others' needs - being selfish.

> That may be true. When we **take care of ourselves,** that sometimes happens. Interestingly though - psychologists tell us others respect us more when we don't allow ourselves to be walked over like a doormat. Our underlying message is: "I respect myself too much to allow this to happen to me."

5. I may do something stupid or show my incompetence. (I'll be sorry later.)

> Begin with needs you're pretty sure will be met. Practice asking for them.
> "Would you get me a cup of coffee?"
> "I would really feel less rushed if you would help me with the dishes."

> Most of us are not in the habit of asking for things we want or need. Practice on little things and grow from there.

ACTIVITY:

Pick one or more of these five beliefs. Design a statement to counteract it. Practice it. Try it. Record your results below.

Assertive vs. Aggressive

It takes kids - and adults - time to learn the difference between assertiveness and aggressiveness. While the person "acting" may be well within the confines of acceptably assertive behavior, the "receiver" may interpret the actions or words as aggressive. Adults who aren't used to children openly expressing their thoughts and wishes will often interpret the child's intent as a power attack.

FAMILY MEETINGS   Stephen Glenn

An excellent method for developing family participation for all ages is the family meeting in which members come together to discuss events, situations, and problems. Each family member is encouraged to participate and everyone listens carefully. This contributes to a child's ability to share and helps to feel that they are important.

Family meetings should be held on a regular basis. The meeting should not be too long or too serious. The responsibility to conduct the meeting is rotated from person to person. The parents start out to provide a model, but even the little ones can learn. Here is a suggested outline to follow until you work out your own:

1. Opening remarks by the person conducting.

2. Review of the family schedule for the upcoming week.

3. Discussion of family business. Anyone can bring up any business.

4. Sharing (This is a time to tell a story, relate experiences, or talk about values or ideas important to the family. Family histories and religious stories are appropriate. Another idea is to spotlight a different family member at each meeting.

5. Activity time (games, singing songs, or whatever the family enjoys.)

6. Refreshments.

CON GAMES

Kids learn to con adults very early - when they're cute!

STAGE 1
Pleading (PLEASE! - PLEASE! - PLEASE!). Designed to wear adults down.

"Please! Can I have just one more cookie?"

"Can I have just one more day to finish my homework?"

"I'll finish when I get back - Honest!!"

STAGE 2
Anger. Designed to generate GUILT.

"You don't care if I flunk Algebra!"

"Teachers never understand how much we have to do!"

Finally, **STAGE 3**

Sulking. Designed to create frustration and anger in the adult.

Off to the room and slam the door!

If we learn to stand firm, kids will eventually give up Con Games because they simply won't be worth the effort.

TIPS TO USE TOMORROW

DEALING WITH CONFLICT

Want to disarm disagreements and build strong relationships?

Here are some ideas from Dr. Robert H. Schuller, author of *Possibility Thinking*.

1. Clarify the issue.

   a. Feelings - mine, theirs
   How do we show these feelings?

   b. Ideas - mine, theirs

   c. Thoughts, beliefs, opinions - mine, theirs

2. Build bridges.

   Solve problems together, one section at a time.
   Building a whole bridge at once may be too much.

3. Generate **patience.**

   Stop! Take time to think about it.
   Take time to let them work it out themselves.
   Recognize steps in the right direction.

4. Foster understanding.

   If you - or they - don't see it the same way, you - or they - must have reasons.
   What are they?

5. Identify weaknesses.

   Do you see any dangers in your approach?

6. Put the other person in your shoes.

   What would you do if.....?
   Try on the other person's shoes.

7. Options.

   What are the alternatives?
   Call in someone else?

8. Reconsider.

   Let's reconsider in light of the new evidence.

ON TELLING THE TRUTH

> "Mom, I really want to be able to tell you
> and Dad what I do in school and with my
> friends. But - it's like, well, I told you about my
> "D" in my history exam yesterday, and you're
> right on me worrying about *all* my grades -
> asking lots of questions and bugging me about
> it. I can't tell you about what I do if that's what's
> going to happen."

Most of us would rather tell the truth. Adults and kids, too! But
often "the truth hurts!"

> The child who breaks a favorite bowl gets a spanking.
> A teenager tells about a date when her boyfriend gets a little
> "handsy" -and Dad declares he's "going to have to talk to
> that boy!"
> An adult gets behind in so many things that a day of "R and
> R" seems to make the most sense - the story to the boss will
> have to be "fudged" a bit.

When asked, teens will tell you that they would like to have their "confidences" -
"truths" treated like they would be if adults were dealing with other adults.

They want to be able to share their lives with the significant adults without
judgement, without imposition of "the way it was in my day", without losing confidence,
and without nagging. It is my experience that teens will ask for advice more often, be
more open in their discussions with adults, and enjoy their relationships with parents
and teachers when "truth" is accepted and dealt with in a "neighborly" way.

WORDS TO EXPRESS FEELINGS

(Brainstorm List generated by 40+ members of Dr. Archer's "Encouragement Process" class in 1977.)

A
agitated
antsy
assertive
at peace
awkward
absurd
accepting
acceptable
accepted
adventuresome
agonize
alive
allowing
aloof
apathetic
appreciative
appreciated
anxious
autonomous
anticipation
away from
appalled
active
alone
afraid
ambitious
angry
athletic
apolitical
ahead

B
bad
bestial
beautiful
belligerent
bitter
blue
bored
bossy
broody
belittled
bashful
babied
bullied
behind
barfy
bereaved

bubbly
burned out

C
capable
carefree
caring
cheerful
charitable
childish
competent
cooperative
crazy
confined
cautious
confident
creative
content
complimentary
complimented
catty
cherished
cared for
cool
concerned
comfortable
comforted

D
disappointed
disheartened
disgusted
discouraged
discouraging
dull
discounted
dependent
daring
dear
determined
dumb
demanding
demeaned
demoralized
depressed
dictatorial
defeated
delighted
distressed

dominating
dopey
down-in-
    the-mouth
drained
dramatic
direct
dishonest
disappointment
disillusioned
disturbed
disoriented

E
effervescent
embarrassed
empathetic
envious
expansive
exploring
exploited
enthusiastic
ecstatic
energetic
emotional
encouraged
encouraging
excited
exciting
eager
elated
enduring
evil
exasperated
exhausted
exuberant

F
fabulous
feminine
freaked out
frugal
fulfilled
furious
futile
foolish
forlorn
fearful
frivolous

free
forgiving
forgiven
formidable
frank
frightened
failure
fat
fooled
frustrated
flexible
flowing
flowering

G
grateful
grieving
grim
guilty
gregarious
grumpy
gullible
generous
gentle
glorius
groupy
greedy
grossed out

H
hurt
helpful
hopeful
hungry
hostile
happy
humiliated
humiliating
heroic
healthy
hyper
heartwarm
happy-go-lucky
humble
helpless
high

I
intelligent
ingenious

ingenuous
incapable
incredulous
inflexible
inquisitive
insignificant
independent
insecure
inferior
intimidated
intimidating
incompetent
insensitive
inconsiderate
impressive
impulsive
inadequate
impatient
innocent
insidious
interested
interesting
incensed

J
jolly
jovial
joyfull
jealous
jumpy
judgemental

K
kinky
kind
kissable

L
lethargic
low
lonely
lovable
loving
loved
loyal
listless
light-hearted
lively
lumpy
left out

lazy
lucky
laid-back
longing
leader
lead

M
miserable
mousy
mad
magnificent
materialistic
mean
mellow
motherly
mysterious
musical
mushy
melancholy

N
neat
nourished
nourishing
needed
needing
never-ending
naughty
nervous
neurotic
normal

O
over-looked
outgoing
optimistic
organized
omnipotent
obnoxious
OK
open
overloaded
overwhelmed

P
pacified
passive
proud
put-upon
parental
patriotic
perfectionistic
persnickity
political

possesive
power-mad
power-hungry
power-drunk
pressured
pretty
persistent
pushed
pushy
patient
pitying
pityful
pleased
powerful
permissive
peaceful
protected
pessimistic
primitive

Q
questionable
questioning

R
regretful
religious
revenge
rejected
removed
rational
resentful
risky
reverent
ridiculous
ridiculed

S
sensitive
surprised
scared
sincere
silly
stingy
satisfied
sympathetic
shy
suicidal
sly
strange
small
sarcastic
sorrowful
sentimental
serious
sad

successful
separate
sexy
sensual
sick
smart
sorry
special
spontanious
serendipitous
stressed
strong
super
supercillious
shocked
sleepy
spacey
squemish
stuckup
sanctimonious

T
terrific
terrified
tactful
tearful
teary-eyed
tricked
taciturn
tacky
tired
tormented
talented
tolerant
touchable
tough
triumphant

U
useless
understanding
unhappy
usual
ugly
unlucky
used
unacceptable
unafraid
unattached
unbalanced
unloved
unloving
unfulfilled
uneasy
unworthy
upset

up-tight
unappreciated
unnoticed

V
valued
victorious
valuable
vulnerable

W
withdrawn
wishy-washy
wrong
weak
with it
witty
worried
worthless
wishful
wasteful
wasted
wanted
warm
weird

X
x-rated
xenophobic

Y
youthful
yearning

Z
zany

— NOTES —

MODULE IV
GOOF AND GROW

THREE CONDITIONS FOR TEACHING SELF-DISCIPLINE AND RESPONSIBILITY

A. **Unqualified Love** + I Love You for who you are, not for what you do!!

B. Clear, specific **feedback** + clear expectations

Try checking (What did you **think** I asked you to do?) when:

1. The child is learning new tasks.

2. You have changed your standards for old tasks.

3. A mistake has been made and change needs to occur.

C. Natural and logical **consequences** + conseqential environment in an atmosphere of **dignity, firmness, and respect.**

Imposed consequences work best:

1. When there is agreement before the situation occurs.
2. When adults are taking care of themselves.
3. When kids know what they are deciding.

Gem

Accuse a kid twice and you'll get the behavior you asked for!

FIVE TRAITS OF A GOOD TEACHER OR PARENT

2 Beliefs

1. Kids are basically good - **people are basically good.**

2. Kids **can** do what we want them to.

3 Skills

1. Have the ability to get on the **kid's feeling level.**

2. Have a **positive self-image**.

3. Have the ability to **be consistent.**

Technique

Your own style for "making your point" and getting cooperation.

Gem

Kids are basically good!

GUIDED PRACTICE WORKSHEET

Describe the Problem:

What is the undesirable behavior?

What would the desired behavior be?

(Make sure each is an observable behavior.)

Is this a problem that your teen acknowledges as his or hers? ---Yes ---No

What do I want him or her to do differently?

How do I want him or her to feel about changing his or her behavior?

Is there a way to meet both of our needs?

What am I willing to do differently?

How do I feel?

What statement will I use to give this problem to my teen?

What is an effective consequence?

Is there a need for further discussion, negotiation, or contracting with my teen for this change?

GUIDE FOR OBSERVERS

Did the teen consider the issue a problem for him or her?

Was the adult able to give the problem to the teen effectively?
(The teen does not have to *like* taking on the problem, just be willing to accept responsibility.)

Was the problem solved in the best way for all involved? (WIN/WIN)

If not, are the adult and teen closer to a solution?

Was each person's self-esteem maintained?

Was open communication established and maintained?

ACTIVITY ASSIGNMENT

Throughout the week, look for the opportunity to use a logical or natural consequence instead of punishment. Describe the situation(s). Check the criteria for using logical consequences on p. 59 in your HANDBOOK. Indicate which of these criteria your logical consequence fits.

How did you feel following the incident?

How did your teen feel?

How do you think your teen will handle a similar situation in the future?

READING ASSIGNMENT

HANDBOOK pp. 77-83

"The Road to Excellence"
"Listening"
"Giving Feelings Credibility"
"Developing Skills in Relationships with Others" by Stephen Glenn

Bonus Reading

HANDBOOK pp. 83-84

"Grounding"
"Preparation for the **REAL** World"

Tips to Use Tomorrow

HANDBOOK pp. 85-89

"Power Stuggles"
"Kids Who Don't Confide"
"She or He's Never with the Family Anymore!"
"Things Adults Ask Kids to Do"

One of the keys to training someone to do something new is to catch him or her doing it *approximately* right.

When children are very young, we **celebrate** their attempts to walk, drink from a cup, tie their shoes, etc. But as children grow older, *we* change.

We tend to disCOURAGE older children by pointing out and sometimes punishing their efforts. For example, if a child is learning to make his bed, what happens when we forget to appreciate the effort and proceed immediately to commenting on the wrinkles? Just a few times of this and no more making the bed. It just doesn't pay off!

How do we react to the teen's room that is cleaner (well, at least a trail to walk through) than it's been in a week? Do they know we noticed and appreciated their effort?

Most people who voluntarily take on a new job are motivated to do the best they can. Think of new people at work. Think of yourself as the new chairman of a committee. How often do we set out to do poorly? Probably NEVER!

We tend to **assume** a teen's intentions are behind the quality of the job.

An alternative to assuming is **checking.**

> What did you think I asked you to do?
> Was I clear about what I wanted?
> Was it possible for you to do it?
> What do I need to teach you so you can do the job?

Teens **assume** too. They assume that they know what you want them to do.

> **Celebrating** movement in the right
> direction, **Checking** for understanding
> and clarification of the **goal** are more
> likely to get the job done the way we
> want it done *eventually*.

Forgetting

Kids have told me that there are times when they "decide to forget" or don't want to do something "right when we ask them" and then they really do forget. They say that trying to meet all of the expectations of all of the adults in their world (parents, teachers, employers) and meet their own needs (friendship, relaxation, fun) is impossible. Discouragement, demotivation, misbehavior, and apathy can set in when the effort to meet our expectations goes unnoticed — when there are more rewards for doing nothing than for doing something.

So how do I reconcile what I need from my teens with what they are doing?

By:

- —Recognizing their efforts in the direction of meeting my needs.
- —Sending "I" messages about my feelings and needs.
- —Understanding and negotiating to meet their needs.
- —Checking and clarifying expectation.
- —Teaching skills needed to do the job the way I expect it to be done.
- —Allowing space for decisions and scheduling of the HOW and WHEN things are to be done.
- —Modeling good work habits, organization, and time management.
- —Having a sense of humor.

LISTENING

Good listening is the foundation of a good relationship. As Ed Frierson mentioned in our third session, messages are sent with **words** and with **body language** (facial expression, tone of voice, posture, and gestures). We "read between the lines" with verbal communication, too.

As we listen, we need to pay attention to two parts of the message:

1. the **content**

2. the **feelings**

Did you ever "listen" to someone while mentally planning what you were going to say next? Did you ever "listen" by **HEARING** the first part of what was said, forming an opinion and letting the rest of the message pass you by? Were you ever introduced to someone whose name you couldn't remember two minutes later?

Good listening requires that we put aside our own reactions and give full **attention** to **all** the **cues** from the other person.

Even when a student catches us in the hall on our way to a class; or even when our teen catches us just as we're on our way out the door to a meeting?

EXAMPLE:

"Wow - you really must have something great to tell me! I'm in a big rush now and won't be able to pay attention. Can we get together at lunch?

Sometimes we have a sixth sense which tells us when a kid wants to talk, but doesn't know how to start. A gesture of a phrase "You look really hassled - want to talk about it?" will "open the door" and let him or her know we're ready and willing to listen.

Keys To Good Listening

Good listening says, "I'm trying my best to understand your feelings and view point, but it is a two-way process." It is a real "turn off" to say "I know how you feel!". It is better to start off with "It sounds like ....." or "Are you saying.....?"

1. Listen for **feelings** and **content**.

2. Listen for **words** and **body language.**

3. Listen with **full attention.**

4. **Look for opportunities** to "open the door" for good listening.

Respond with **acceptance** and an effort to **understand feelings** and **point of viewing.**

5. Accept the feelings and/or point of viewing without judgement.

6. Because listening requires **interpretation** of the message, it is possible to interpret wrong.

Good listening *requires* that we *check out* our interpretation. Good listening is *not* mind reading.

EXAMPLE:

Mom: "You sound really upset with your Math teacher."

Sally: "I'm really angry because ....."

Or she might say,
"No. I guess I'm really upset with myself for making so many dumb mistakes."

GIVING FEELINGS CREDIBILITY

John: "That teacher is just out to get me. I hate school!"

Dad: "Now John, calm down. You know you don't really hate school."

There are a lot of **feelings** behind John's words. What did the Dad's response do to those feelings?

We all need to be able to feel what we feel and express it appropriately. As adults we also need to accept the validity of children's feelings.

EXAMPLE:

When John says: "Girls are all *so* stupid!"

Restrain yourself from saying, "That's not true!
Some girls are really quite bright."

When we forget to **deal** with the **feelings** of the message, we make **assumptions** about children's reasoning, their ability to understand situations clearly, and their right to have strong feelings about their world.
As a result, we find ourselves in conflict without any understanding of how we got there or why this strong reaction.

Ways To Give Teens' Feelings Credibility;

1. Don't deny the teen's feelings:

EXAMPLE:

Teen: "Going to Grandma's is so boring!"

Mom: "You shouldn't feel like that. You know Grandma loves you."

Teen: "I just hate going over there!"

Mom: (In frustration)"OK, just don't go then!"

Instead Give the Feelings Names:

EXAMPLE:

Teen: "Going to Grandma's is so boring!

Mom: "I know there really isn't much for you to do there. Grandma enjoys seeing you so much, though."

Teen: "Yeh, I just sit around and listen to adults talk!"

Mom: "You feel sort of left out. Like no one knows you're there? Ignored?"

Teen: "Yeh."

Mom: "Well, maybe we can make a better effort to include you in more of the conversation."

2. Don't pay only half attention:

EXAMPLE:

Teacher: (Continuing to grade a paper) "You don't feel the grade on your test is fair?"

Teen: "My answer is almost exactly the same as Sara's."

Teacher: (Still grading.) "Oh?"

Teen: "Yeh, I have..... and she had the same thing. You counted hers right and mine wrong"

Teacher: (Never looking up from the grading.) "Humm-m-m."

Teen: (Angry and frustrated.) "Oh, never mind! You never listen to me anyway!"

Instead Listen With Full Attention:

Teacher: (Looking at student, perhaps even with a friendly smile) "You don't feel the grade on your test is fair?"

Teen: (Bringing paper around the desk for teacher to see.) "My answer is almost exactly the same as Sara's."

Teacher: (Looking at the answer, and then turning to the teen to respond.) "You're right, it is similar. However, I was looking for this additional information. I believe Sara included it in her answer." (Smile, eye contact.)

Teen: "Oh, OK."

3. Don't deal only with the content and ignore the feelings:

EXAMPLE:

Teen: "Jane is such a creep! She told all the girls I was cheating on my Math test!"

Adult: "Well, maybe you should be careful. Were you cheating?"

Teen: "I wasn't even looking at her paper. Why would I want to do that?"

Adult: "Teachers really have to watch out for cheating. You'll just have to be more careful - keep your eyes on your own paper!"

Teen: "Oh, you never understand!"

Instead Listen Without Questions or Advice:

EXAMPLE:

Teen: "Jane is such a creep! She told all the girls I was cheating on my Math test."

Adult: "Oh, you're angry with her?"

Teen: "She makes me so mad. She's just jealous because I get better grades."

Adult: "Hum-m-m. I wonder if that's it?"

Teen: "Well, I was looking her way, but I didn't cheat."

Adult: "Hum-m-m."

Teen: "Well, I won't even look her way next time!"

4. Don't judge the feelings as unimportant:

EXAMPLE:

Teen: "I wish I didn't have to go to the dentist."

Adult: "Well, you know you have to so quit worrying about it!"

Instead Give The Feelings Credibility

EXAMPLE:

Teen: "I wish I didn't have to go to the dentist."

Adult: "Dentists do worry people sometimes. Those drills can really hurt."

Teen: "Yeh, but I guess a toothache would hurt worse."

DEVELOPING SKILLS IN RELATIONSHIPS WITH OTHERS   Stephen Glenn

Interpersonal skills can be used to develop friendships, establish the deep and intimate human relationships we all crave, and validate our identity.

Interpersonal skills start with the ability to carry on a conversation, but there are many more which are deeper and more complex. They include the ability to share ideas and feelings, to sense the feelings and needs of others, to be able to listen to others, and to give and receive love. Also included are skills like cooperation, empathy, negotiation, and sharing.

The cluster of interpersonal skills hinges on the adequacy of listening skills. The ability to listen is particularly important for a parent or a leader of youth. Nothing makes a five-year-old feel more important than to be listened to. Nothing creates a rift between parents and teenagers faster than lack of listening on the parent's part. Unfortunately, many teenagers have been lectured to for so many years that they develop an automatic "tune-out" capability.

How many parents have been told by a teenage son or daughter that they "just don't understand." This message, when decoded or "unpacked," usually means something like this.

Teenager: "I am in a situation where I have strong feelings. I don't think you appreciate the fact that I'm older and that I have the ability and the **developmental need** to think through a problem and come to an independent conclusion. I don't need your help on this one. My experience and my feelings are obviously not appreciated or understood by you or you wouldn't be standing there telling me these things."

Parent: "I know exactly what you are saying and how you feel because I was exactly the same way. However, with my 20-20 hindsight, my current set of values, and my insight on the world, I now see that what matters to you shouldn't matter to you. Here, look at it through my 40-year-old eyes and with my 40-year-old values. Forget having 16-year-old values and feelings because they are shallow and hollow. Mine are better and you should adopt them. Being 16 is no excuse for acting like a 16-year-old."

Teenager: "You just don't understand." (You don't listen, you don't learn, you don't care.)

These interchanges almost always put distance between parents and teenagers.

What is the solution? Listen - truly listen - to what the child has to say. Advice given sparingly is valued more because it is rarely given and therefore has a premium quality to it. Listening is also an excellent way to develop interpersonal skills and relationships.

BONUS READING

GROUNDING

The authority we use with adolescents is positive when it means to influence, permit, and give responsibility. This same authority becomes negative control when it means to regulate, contain, manipulate, or direct. Grounding is usually an attempt to exercise negative control.

My children often tell me, "John can't go. He's grounded again!"

"Why was he grounded?"

"Oh, he stayed out too late."
or
"His grades weren't good enough."
or
"He sassed his Dad."
or
"He didn't get his chores done."

Review your criteria for logical consequences on p. 59. Think about why grounding is not a logical consequence for these examples.

Two tips for grounding:

1. Ask yourself: "Am I robbing my teen of the opportunity to trust his or her own judgement and learn from this experience?"

Make a list of times you have used grounding. Could these situations have been handled in another way?

2. Kids want limits. They also want input into those limits. When you have agreed that "Work will come before play" or "Midnight is a reasonable time to expect me home" or "I'll give you a call when we have decided where we're going", the teen has the choice "to do or not to do". Grounding becomes "deciding to stay in the next three nights" when the agreement is not met. The problem and the decision are the teen's.

PREPARATION FOR LIFE

If we want to prepare our kids for the real world, the home and the school must operate like the real world.

Thousands of kids miss the school bus every day. But people don't often miss a plane. What's the difference? The way it's handled! We know the airline won't call the flight back.

Parents of adolescents are constantly feeling used.

EXAMPLE:

Kids borrow money, promise to repay it, and then let the payment slide. In fact, I've even said to myself, "Well, I know Scott's broke, and he wants to take Jill to Homecoming. Oh, well, I can just let it slide."

In the real world, how would the bank handle this situation? First, we usually have to put up collateral for a loan. Then, there is interest (encouragement to pay it back sooner). And, there is a loan due date. If we fail to take care of our debts, our credit rating goes, and we have a hard time borrowing in the future.

If you're feeling used, ask yourself, "How would this be handled in the real world?"

TIPS TO USE TOMORROW

POWER STRUGGLES

When conflict occurs between an adult and a child, it centers around the question, "Who is more powerful?" Children, seeking to control their own world (adults included), will challenge authority by ignoring or breaking rules. Our tendency, as adults, is to react to the challenge and feel we must force compliance or lose control. The power game is on. Even if we win, we are reinforcing the belief that it's only power that gets results.

When you sense a power struggle on the way, try to avoid it!

Some useful strategies:

A. Fantasize wishes

"I have so much homework I'll never get it done!"

"I'll bet you wish you didn't have to do it." (Instead of offering "logical" advice about how to get it done.)

B. Fogging (Agreeing in concept with the teen without changing the ground rules)

"That isn't fair! Sally only had to make up two reports when she was sick!"

"It may seem that way to you *and* I'll expect you to turn in all your make up work."

C. Repeat (Broken record)

John:	"I don't know what we're supposed to do."
Teacher:	"I gave the instructions before you arrived. You'll have to get them after class."
John:	"I was only a few minutes late. How am I gonna' get my work done?"
Teacher:	"I gave the instructions before you arrived. You'll have to get them after class."
John:	"That's not fair! You helped Sally a minute ago."

Teacher:	"I gave the instructions before you arrived. You'll have to get them after class."
John:	"I told my Mom you wouldn't help me!"
Teacher:	"I gave the instructions before you arrived. You'll have to get them after class."
John:	"Oh , all right! When can I get some help?"
Teacher:	"I'll be happy to help you right after class."

D. Deal with the feelings

Jeff:	"That teacher is such a jerk!" (Slamming pencil down on the desk.)
Parent:	"You sound upset."
Jeff:	"Yeh. I'm gonna' drop that class. I hate Geometry anyway! And you can't make me take it!"
Parent:	"Something make you angry?"
Jeff:	"Jenkins gives us assignments and never explains anything!"
Parent:	"As soon as you feel a bit calmer, why don't we take a look at it?"

E. "Tame the angry tiger"
(The trick is to use feeling words of less emotional value with each response.)

Sally:	"Do you know what Jennifer did to me? She spilled chocolate all over the sweater I loaned her and she didn't even try to clean it out! I'll never speak to her again!"
Mom:	"I'll bet you're really *mad!*"
Sally:	"Well, it was my favorite sweater!"
Mom:	"You're *angry* about her thoughtlessness."

Sally:	"She'll never borrow anything of mine again!"
Mom:	"The damage is reason to be *upset*."
Sally:	"Yeh, I don't know if it will ever come out."
Mom:	"You'll *probably feel better* if we can get it out."
Sally:	"Do we have some spot remover?"

E. Avoid the Conflict

If other strategies are not going to work, ask yourself,

"Is this something I really do control?"

If the answer is "yes", then win it! If the answer is "no", then stay out of it. This problem belongs on the "kid's pile".

****

KIDS WHO DON'T CONFIDE

Little children always tell us their secret feelings, but adolescents no longer seem to have that need. And yet, we, as adults, want to continue the closeness we used to feel.

Several things happen that change the adolescent's ability to confide in us. At the time we want to know how a teen feels about something, s/he may still be trying to sift and sort reactions and feelings. Sometimes, teens have figured out how they're feeling but don't know how to express those feelings without appearing "stupid".

Another block is that teens have thoughts and opinions they know will not agree with those of their parents. They don't want to open disagreement, even if their relationship is good.

Give teens the space they need to work out their thoughts and feelings. At the same time, be available when they need you. It's a tough line to follow but, well done, the relationship between you and your teen will grow and flourish as it would with a friend.

S/HE'S NEVER WITH THE FAMILY ANYMORE!

"I can't find a night to get the whole family together anymore!" laments Mom.

"We don't go places together much, anymore!" complains Dad.

Teens are truly busy. They spend time with school, friends, jobs, and athletics. They also spend some time alone. If you did all of these things every day, how much time would you have with your family? Not much!

"But," say Mom and Dad, "even when s/he has time, it's not spent with the family!"

Very often true. Adolescence is a time of growing away from the family. While the teen's job is to become independent, the parents are counting the few years left at home! Conflicts develop frequently over this issue.

Try to understand your teen's need to spend time away from the family. Treasure those times when s/he is there and know that "growing away" is healthy.

****

THINGS ADULTS ASK KIDS TO DO TO MAKE THEM FEEL LISTENED TO, TAKEN SERIOUSLY AND GENUINELY NEEDED

(Compiled from responses given by several classes of kids)

1. Do laundry because kids are not always trusted to do this important job.

2. Wait on adults.

3. Do things not everyone is trusted to do.

4. Plan menus and help with the grocery shopping.

5. Help with the housework, yard, fix dinner, take care of pets.

6. Care for neighbor's pets, house sit, special jobs, shovel snow.

7. Explain about computers to parents.

8. Have adult-type conversations with parents about news, world affairs, etc.

9. Babysit with siblings.

10. Help make things - dinner - fix things (younger boys especially want to help Dad make things out of wood, nail things, etc.)

11. Help younger kids.

12. Start in games.

13. Be allowed to be their own person.

14. Run errands. Example: Take money to the bank.

15. Make more of his or her own decisions regarding curfew, picking out own clothes, etc.

16. Be left at home while parents go on vacation or are gone for a weekend.

17. Take kid's plans into consideration.

18. Translate teen lingo, music, fads.

19. When kids are really listened to and are asked their advice and/or opinions.

20. Take friends along on vacations and be allowed their own hotel room.

21. Chauffeur others around town, etc.

22. Make and take important phone calls.

23. Help when Dad needs four hands and strength.

24. Clean out the fireplace and then make a fire in it.

(Ask your kids what makes THEM feel Listened to, Taken Seriously, and Genuinely needed.)

25.

26.

27.

28.

29.

30.

MODULE V
THE KID NEXT DOOR

Gem

Success does not mean never falling down.
It means getting up and trying again.

Communication involves two major elements:

1. The sharing of ideas and feelings.

2. Hearing thoughtfully and helping to explore what the other person is trying to communicate.

Good Listening Requires

Full **attention**

Warmth and **acceptance**
(Eye contact, smiles, and touching)

Patience

Feelings Expressed in Gestures

BODY LANGUAGE   POSSIBLE FEELINGS

Tears

Slamming things

Smiling

Yawning

Arms folded tightly, eyes
looking down at the floor

Touching on the arm

Leaning forward attentively

Sitting comfortably, looking relaxed

Head nodding, eyes almost closed

****

We disregard teens feelings when we

1. Deny that the feelings exist or should exist.

2. Offer advice which ignores the feelings and deals only with the content.

3. Listen while really paying attention to something else.

4. Judge the feelings as unimportant.

We can attend to kids' feelings by:

      1. Giving Feelings NAMES.

      2. Listening with Full ATTENTION.

      3. Listening without Questions or Advice.

      4. Giving Feelings Credibility.

Our Self-image changes because of:

      1. New information

      2. New experiences

Self-Image comes from:

      1. What we believe about what others tell us (parents and other adults).

      2. Grades in school.

      3. Boy/Girl dynamics (friendship dynamics).

Gem

Treat your teen like he or she belongs to the neighbors.

OBSERVER'S WORKSHEET

GENERAL DESCRIPTION OF THE SITUATION:

ADULT'S POSITION:

CHILD'S POSITION:

OBJECTIVES FOR THE CONVERSATION/CONFRONTATION:

Clarify and define the end result desired. (Use four basic questions.)

1. **WHAT** do you want done differently?

2. **HOW** do you want the other person to **FEEL?**

3. **WHAT** are you willing to **DO** differently?

4. **HOW** do I **FEEL?**

—After the Conversation—

REVIEW:

DID THE ADULT:
Determine the nature of the conflict?
Hear and value the child's point of view?
Use problem solving skills to achieve a Win/Win resolution?
Contract for a behavior change?

Evaluate the Conversation/Confrontation.

yes   no

yes	no	
_____	_____	Was the problem solved in the best way for both of us?
_____	_____	If not, are we closer to a solution?
_____	_____	Was the person's self-esteem maintained?
_____	_____	Was open communication maintained?
_____	_____	Was the contract truly agreed upon by both?

ACTIVITY ASSIGNMENT

Review all of the information you have about talking with teens so they'll listen and listening so they'll talk.

Look for an opportunity to talk with your teen about something: a problem, something you are pleased with, something that you see the teen doing that concerns you, even though you know it is his or her problem, a situation you handled poorly the first time and now you think you can smooth it over, etc.

Then talk with your teen. (I hope you have remembered the RULES FOR LEARNING on page xv. Don't pick a problem that will wipe you and your teen out if something goes wrong.)

Briefly describe the situation.

Describe your feelings.

Describe what you think your teen is feeling.

What would you like to see happen? If it did, what are some of the consequences for you? For your teen?

What do you want to say?

How can your teen be involved in the decision?

What are the consequences if there is no change in the situation?

Record the results below. Be prepared to discuss them at our next session.

READING ASSIGNMENT

HANDBOOK pp. 97-104

"Encouraging Self-Esteem"
"Praise"
"Contracts"

Bonus Reading

HANDBOOK pp. 104-106

"Adjustment As a Game Process" by Ed Frierson
"It's Hard to Get My Kids to 'Pitch In' and Help"
"Units of Worry"

Tips to Use Tomorrow

HANDBOOK pp. 107

"Giving Advice"
"Giving Effective Feedback"

ENCOURAGING SELF-ESTEEM

That illusive shadow of me---

I have a little shadow that
Goes in and out with me.

But what can be the use of him
Is more than I can see.

He is very, very like me
From my head down to my toes -

What is it? This Self-Esteem?

That intricately woven concept of feelings, fears, strengths, and emotions that comes to form a mirror of my experience, past and present...

That filtered, shaded view of the "real" me.

That image which so strongly affects the way I approach the world and tomorrow.

Our self-concept grows and changes as we grow and change. It develops through our thoughts about how others see and react to us. As situations change, so does our image of ourselves.

EXAMPLES:

A 6'4", 210 lb. football lineman may be a real hero during the game on Tuesday night. He made the tackle that stopped the kick! It was the crucial play of the game! The Knights win 14-13! Into the locker room on the shoulders of his buddies.

But Wednesday morning, he's at the back of the History class, slumped down in his chair, struggling to remember that list of names and dates he had studied so hard. "Why can't I remember those things?" he thinks to himself.

*****

Susan walks in the door, "Mom, I've done it! I just landed a date with the cutest boy. Wow!"

"That's nice, Susan. I thought I asked you to clean your room before you left for school!"

Self-esteem - How do we get it from the environment?

Positive self-esteem comes from an environment in which we are listened to, taken seriously, and genuinely needed. Positive self-esteem gives us meaning and purpose for our lives. It makes us feel significant and provides relevance in our relationships. It gives us confidence and status. It supports feelings of being capable and encourages independence.

A woman walked into my office recently to discuss her divorce. "Why is it," she said, "that it took me until I was 35 years old to discover I can make decisions that are good for me? That I can take care of myself?"

What happens as we are growing up that leads us to believe we are inadequate, powerless, unappreciated, unable to contribute, and unable to influence what happens to us?

PRAISE

"Terrific job!" "Wonderful!" "Good work."

How often we often give and receive this type of praise. When we praise this way, we assume:

1. The person being praised picks up on our pleasure and appreciates our evaluation, and

2. Our evaluation of the effort fits with what the person actually did.

— 98 —

Mary Budd Rowe, a University of Florida professor, has done research in the area of praise; its effects on children and what they learn, how they learn, and their attitudes about learning. She has found that:

1. We don't praise all children equally.

2. Praise teaches children that learning's rewards come from external sources (teachers and parents) rather than developing from the satisfaction inherent in the learning itself.

3. Praise conditions people to go for a "quick payoff".

4. Praise is a method of control to get others to do what we want them to do. This is particularly true when we begin to believe our worth depends on the opinions of others. Praise can actually lead to discouragement. What if we are dependent on praise for our feelings of self-worth, but are seldom PRAISE worthy? Fear of not meeting expectations can lead to just "giving up".

Teachers and psychologists have found praise doesn't work well with resistant children or people with low self-esteem.

A teacher says, "I praised John this morning for doing such a good job, and he blew it this afternoon!" Psychologists explain that "blowing it" is a result of cognitive dissonance, which means the **praise** doesn't fit with John's self-image!

In effect, John is telling the teacher, "You say I'm terrific! I know I'm not. So, I'll prove it!"

So what do we do instead?

We can simply state our pleasure without evaluation.

"Wow - you have really made me happy!"

"I really like that!"·

"I really appreciate this!"

If we want teens to learn to evaluate their own efforts, instead of telling them they've done a good job, we can say:

"How do *you* feel about this?"

Most of the time the response will be, "OK", or "Pretty good". If the response is, "I think I did a great job!" it's quite safe to add, "I really like it, too." We've allowed the teen to take the lead and own the pleasure for his or her efforts.

What if we ask, "How do you feel about this?" and the teen replies, "Not so good." Here again we can respond in a way which allows the teen to own his or her own feelings, too.

"Well, considering the result, I can certainly understand."

"Oh?"

"Well, I hope it goes better next time."

"Bummer."

Sometimes a "surprise/ shocked" approach works well:

EXAMPLE:

> Amy's papers are usually messy but today she turns in a neat one. The teacher smiles, looks Amy squarely in the eye and says, "You?! Did this?"

> Then Amy can smile and say to herself, "Yeh, I'm usually pretty messy, but today I did a good job!"

> When you want to tell someone they have done a good job:

> 1. State specifically what they've done. "You got all ten problems right! That's one more right than yesterday!" Or "The colors in your painting really describe the tone of the day!" Or "Blue is a lovely color on you."

> 2. Use this "praise" sparingly!

CONTRACTS

Contracts are **joint** agreements between people to accomplish something.

EXAMPLES:

> Sheila agrees to have her room cleaned once a week, by noon on Saturday. Mom agrees not to "bug" her about it the rest of the week. She will just shut the door.

> ***************

Arthur agrees to complete his late homework by tomorrow noon. The teacher agrees to accept it.

Contracts are common in business. They can be very useful at home and school if:

> 1. All parties agree to the terms.

> 2. The teen values the benefits which can occur.

> Contracts include statements about the action to be taken and the performance of the contract will be evaluated.

When .... happens, I will .... (do something different) instead (of what I do now.)

Psychologists have found that two things seem to affect the likelihood of people's commitment to action in a contract.

1. If we say aloud what we are willing to do.

> "I understand that I am responsible for doing my homework and turning it in on time. I will do it each evening before I watch television."

For us to verbalize the contract and teens to say "yes" doesn't provide the commitment.

We need to say *our* half of the contact and the teen needs to say what he or she has agreed to do.

2. If we sign our name, we feel more compelled to do what we said we'd do once it is in writing.

It is also useful to set time limits and check back to see how things are going.

In order to arrive at a contract both parties can commit to, we have to make sure we have listened to and understood each other. Conflict management experts have another little trick that helps communication during discussion of a problem. They suggest each person repeat what the other is saying in their own words.

EXAMPLES:

Dad: "I really get upset when I find my tools rusting out in the yard because I know I will have to spend extra time cleaning them in order to make them useful again."

Bob: (Repeats what he's heard.) "You get upset when you see your tools rusting because they have to be cleaned before you can use them again."

Dad: "Yes , that's what I said." (Verifies that's what he meant.)

****

Eric: "You always yell at me about not getting the yard work done. I feel like you expect me to do it all by myself, and I don't think that's fair. I have other things to do, too."

Mom: (Repeats what she's heard.) "You don't think it's fair for you to have to do all the yard work by yourself because you have other things to do, too."

Eric:	"Yeh! Saturday afternoon is the only free time I have. I want to spend some of my weekend with my friends."
Mom:	"You feel picked on because no one else has to work so long?"
Eric:	"I do. Susan is big enough to help with some of the work. If I had help I could get done sooner."
Mom:	"With Susan to help, you'd have more time for your friends."
Eric:	"Yeah."
Mom:	"How shall we get Susan to help?"
Eric:	"Maybe you could make a list of the jobs to be done and Susan and I could sign up each week. That way we'd know what you wanted done and you'd know who was supposed to do it."
Mom:	"Good idea. Let's make the list for next Saturday."

At school, we contract primarily for behavior change. Even grades are a form of contract if teens know the requirements for A, B, C, D and so on. We also contract for make-up work and classroom behavior.

When Contracting with Teens, Keep in Mind:

Contracts are **joint agreements**.

Adults and teens must see the need, **want to change, and appreciate the benefits** of that change.

Teens need to be **involved** in deciding how the contract is going to work.

A contract should include a clear understanding of the problem by all involved with **acceptance** of **responsibility** by those who can solve the problem.

A contract should include a **commitment** for **action** and **evaluation** of performance. This means some standards have to be set.

Time Out In Schools

Time Out is one of the ways schools use to control behavior in the classroom. It works better when the teacher and the student have established a "contract" about the use of Time Out.

In a conversation with a teen who may need "time out" from your classroom, several ideas are helpful.

Teachers are responsible for:

A. Taking care of themselves so they can do their best teaching.

B. Taking care of the other students so they can do their best learning.

EXAMPLE:

Teacher: "Time Out is a place we have in the building for students to go who are not ready to learn right now. I send students to Time Out when my teaching is being disturbed or when other students' learning is being disturbed. Can you tell when you are disturbing my teaching or others' learning?"

Lisa: "Yeah."

Teacher: "I don't want to embarass you by sending you to Time Out and calling the rest of the students' attention to it. Is there a way that I can signal you to let you know you should go to Time Out?"

Lisa: "You could come by and touch me on the shoulder."

Teacher: "When I do that, there are two ways you can respond. You can make a fuss or you can go quietly. Which would you rather do?"

Lisa: "Go quietly."

Teacher: "How long do you think that you should stay in Time Out?"

Lisa: "Until I am ready to learn?"

Teacher: "Not necessarily. Whose problem is it whether you learn or not?"

Lisa: "Mine?"

Teacher: "Right. Why is it that you will be asked to go to the Time Out room?"

Lisa: "Because I am disturbing your teaching or the other kids' learning."

Teacher:	"Right. Now, when do you think you should come back from Time Out?"
Lisa:	"When I won't bother your teaching anymore or the other kids' learning."
Teacher:	"That sounds good. Now, there are two ways to return to the classroom. One is loudly. The other is slipping in quietly. Which one will you do?"
Lisa:	"Come in quietly."
Teacher:	"OK. Now we both know what to do when you feel like disturbing the class."

Gem

The only half of the relationship I control is my half.

BONUS READING

ADJUSTMENT AS A GAME PROCESS adapted by Ed Frierson

Feedback on performance is a key issue. In most of life's crucial games we stumble in the dark, not knowing how we are doing. The first step, then, in behavior change is explicit definition of the game, learning the roles, rules, rituals, language, values, and strategies. We need some way of scorekeeping, and we have to study the space-time locale and be at the proper ball park. We aren't going to be creative if we share our space/time with salesmen.

We must be sure to have an explicit contract with our colleagues. It is disappointing to come thundering over the goal line for a touchdown only to be greeted with yawns because the gang is playing tennis. We tend to do this all the time.

We should get a good coach. Behavior, being movement in space/time, is not changed by words and is not changed by repeating mistakes. Practice is needed.

The general procedure is as follows: The subject picks out a goal and practices the game sequences which lead to success. The goal must be behavioral and capable of measurement. Much confusion is caused because people engage in games for which there is no way of scorekeeping. Is the game over when the New York Yankees "feel" they have won? Suppose that the Detroit Tigers "feel" they have won, too. Suppose the scoreboard shows that the Tigers won, but they or their supporters "feel" they lost. The movements in space/time (men crossing home plate) have to be the criterion.

-Leary, 1964-

Suppose we set out to improve our playing of the Mother Game, the Professor Game, the Daughter Game, the Student Game, the Well-Adjusted Good Ol' Boy Game. Which games could we coach for our teens?

IT'S HARD TO GET MY KIDS TO "PITCH IN" AND HELP!

Also known as getting kids to cooperate with us and with each other.

Years ago we were expected to work. Chores were necessary to the survival of the family. We were willing to work because everyone else did. In today's largely urban society, jobs are not so clearly related to family survival as when eggs had to be gathered, gardens weeded, and the animals fed. Dads, and often Moms, go off to work, but teens rarely see them at work.

Ask a teen to describe the benefits of a "clean room", "walking the dog", or "cleaning up the kitchen after dinner". The answer would probably be a short, "I don't know!"

Adolescents who are not college bound are hard pressed to see the value of much of what is taught at school. Showing up at all may be valuable only as a way to stay out of trouble with the law!

PEOPLE DO WHAT THEY DO (INCLUDING KIDS) IN ORDER TO GET SOMETHING **THEY** WANT!

Thus, getting kids to cooperate or pitch in boils down to rewards, bribes, or incentives.

It is not my intent to encourage BRIBES. Bribes are paying someone to do something that is either dishonest or isn't good for him or her. But the "real world" operates on the basis of rewards and incentives. Businesses know that money may be the reason we take jobs, but once the contract is in place, it is not the major reason we do a good job. The "pay off" for a job well done is satisfaction.

Incentives for teens include:

1. Having their opinions, choices, ideas included in the development and assignment of work.

2. Being genuinely needed - contributing in a meaningful way.

3. Receiving appreciation, affection, attention.

4. Being recognized for a job well done or for efforts toward doing well (often accompanied by specific feedback on the quality of the task).

5. Being allowed choices in how and when the job is done.

6. Being able to work along side us - this can mean physically working with them or rooting for them and providing support when asked.

7. Receiving a trade off or contracting. ("If I do some extra credit work, will you raise my grade?" "If I clean up the kitchen will you wash a load of my jeans?" "I can take you to your potluck meeting, if you can help me finish the lawn.")

9. Being paid. (Kids' expenses rise as they grow older. They need to learn to "earn" the extras.)

UNITS OF WORRY

"No sense in both of us worrying about it" syndrome.

When parents and teachers worry about things that are really the kids' problems (grades, clean clothes, what to wear when it's cold out, whom to choose for friends, how to spend their allowance) kids think, "Hm-m, I guess if they're going to worry about that. I don't need to!"

Who worries about the laundry at your house? Who worries about having food in the house for meals and snacks? Who worries about having enough books for each student in class?

When you are taking a trip with someone else, who does the driving? Who is the navigator? What if you make a wrong turn? Or can't find the address or place you're going? Whose fault is it if you wander around for an hour looking for something you can't find? Who was supposed to worry about it? Not me! Oh!

At our house my husband is supposed to worry about keeping the cars in repair so they don't break down when I'm driving. Let's suppose we allocated ten **units of worry** for the problem "Keeping the cars running". Who has all the units of worry? My husband, supposedly.

On the first cold day last winter, I saw smoke coming out of the hood of my car. I knew my car had over-heated. I knew because it did the same thing last year and my husband had fixed it!

This time, I called him. There was no answer. Fortunately, I was near a gas station and I had watched how he had fixed the car before. The problem solved, I went on my way.

In terms of units of worry, how many do you suppose I might take relative to anti-freeze in the cars? Three? Five? You're right! I could get the anti-freeze and "hint" about putting it in. I could just "remind" several 100 times. I could even do it myself and take all the units of worry.

How many units of worry do you think my husband will take for the car now that he knows I'll take them for myself? Probably none.

That's what happens with kids when we worry about their problems. Nagging, anger, rescuing, reminders, all let them believe their problem is our problem. Their ten units of worry become ours. How many units of worry does your teen carry for misbehaving, driving fast, denting the car, cleaning his or her room, etc.

"But," you say, "I worry about things that will affect his or her whole life!" When s/he leaves home, who will worry about those things? If teens decide not to take care of themselves, can we make them - really?

If our goal is to "develop independent, capable young people" our children must take the responsibility for worrying about their problems early in life! The *only* way to get them to take this responsibility is **not** to take the **units of worry** ourselves!

TIPS TO USE TOMORROW

GIVING ADVICE

Rule of Thumb: Never give advice unless it is requested.

What? Never? No, never! Instead share your own thoughts, feelings, ideas, experiences in a manner similar to a consultant. This often leads to a request for advice about "What should I do?" **Sharing** thoughts and opinions leaves the decision to your teen.

Did you appreciate the advice you received before your first baby was born? The advice from well-meaning friends when you bought your car? Or moved into your home, chose your church, changed jobs?

Teens don't either. They are working very hard to develop their identity which includes learning to make decisions. Those who come from protective environments where most of the thinking is done for them react to advice by:

1. Rebelling and resisting adult efforts to influence them.
2. Capitulating and not being able to resist peer pressure, cult leaders, etc.

If you blow it, do you expect me to lecture you about it? Of course not. I might think something, but I won't say anything. Why? Because you haven't asked me. It's important to treat kids the same way.

However, by using DIALOG, we can help teens give themselves advice.

1. WHAT happened?
2. WHAT was important about the experience?
3. WHAT MAKES it important?
4. HOW can you use this information in the future?

GIVING EFFECTIVE FEEDBACK

As we coach, or give teens feedback, we should:

1. Describe, not judge.

2. Be specific and direct our comments to the task.

3. Talk about now, not the past.

4. Respect the teen's right *not* to change.

5. Describe the deed, not the doer.

6. Respect the teen's ability to "appreciate" the information.

MODULE VI
ENCOURAGEMENT

We don't **pursue** happiness. We must have a **reason** to be **happy**.

-Victor Frankl-

****

Meaning, purpose, and significance in our lives comes from the feeling that we are:

1. Listened to and **understood.**

2. **Taken seriously, given unqualified love**, positive regard, and **respect**.

3. Genuinely **needed**, we play an important role in the lives of others.

****

THE IMPORTANCE OF SUCCESS*

"...recent research on teaching makes a contribution by showing that students require a very high success rate in order to progress efficiently. Theoretical sources vary on this point. The achievement motivation literature suggests that a 50% success rate is optimal for maximizing achievement motivation, at least for individuals who do not fear failure (Crawford, 1978), and this finding has sometimes been appropriately generalized and transformed into a notion that classroom questions and assignments should be geared to a 50% success rate. Similarly, writers who believe that higher level of 'thought' questions are more valuable than lower level of 'fact' questions frequently state or imply that learning which is 'too easy' is likely to be repetitive, boring, or pointless. On the other hand, mastery learning advocates usually demand at least 80% success on assignments and tasks, and programmed learning advocates expect to approach 100%. Classroom data support the latter position, indicating that teachers who program for 90-100% success rates on student assignments produce better student learning than teachers who tolerate higher failure rates (Fisher, et al., 1980.)'

What changes would you need to make to program for 90-100% success?

*Brophy, Jere, RESEARCH ON TEACHING, Michigan State University. Paper delivered to the annual meeting of the Northeastern Educational Research Association, October, 1980.

What causes **disCOURAGEment**?

> Excessively high standards.
>
> Negative expectations.
>
> Subtle competition.
>
> Overly ambitious adults.
>
> Pampering.

The **ANTIDOTE? EnCOURAGEment**

> Focus on what's **right**.
>
> Have **positive** expectations.
>
> **Value them as they are.**
>
> **Trust** them.
>
> Build their **self-respect**.
>
> Value **their** goals.
>
> Give them **freedom of choice** and the **opportunity** to learn from **consequences**.
>
> Help them feel **significant**.
>
> Recognize their **efforts**.
>
> Look for **assets**.
>
> Maintain our sense of **humor**.

Gem

Teens need encouragement the same way plants need water.

- Rudolph Dreikurs -

PRAISE something OUTSTANDING!

ENCOURAGE movement in a FORWARD direction!

REPLACE THESE DISCOURAGING STATEMENTS WITH ENCOURAGING ONES

1. (Sara has just finished preparing dinner.)
Mom asks, "What's all this mess in the kitchen?"

2. (John has just brought home his report card. He got four "A's", one "B", and one "C".)
His dad looks at the report card and says, "A 'C'?"

3. (Terri tries to help by washing the family car.)
Dad comments, "Thanks for washing the car, Terri. How come you didn't wash the hubcaps?"

4. (Tina has just cleaned her room. It is the first time she has done it by the time her Mother asked her to get it done.)
Mom says, "What's all that stuff under your bed?"

5. (Scott has finally finished his term paper. He spent a lot of hours doing the research and thinking about how to say what he wanted to in the paper. The teacher has just returned the paper "graded". It is full of red marks and a grade of "F".)
The only comment: "Your spelling is awful!"

6. (Chris is trying to get her teacher to explain something she doesn't understand.)
The teacher says, "Didn't your teacher teach you that last year?"

7. (Barbara has baked a cake because her Dad is coming home after being away for a long trip.)
Mom says, "Your cake sure does look lopsided. What happened?"

8. (Mike asks his Dad to help him change the oil in his car for the first time).
Dad says, "Here, I'll do it."

PLANNING FOR BEHAVIORAL CHANGE

What's the Problem? Description	What do I do When it Happens?	What do I Want my Teen to do?	What are 3 Things that are really NEAT about (Name)	What will I do instead?

Tips: Remember, the ONLY ½ of the Relationship we truly control is OUR ½!

You may never have really told your teens things that are really NEAT about him or her. Remember, when you are talking about things in that column, it is VERY DIScouraging to say, "You're really neat, BUT ..."

CONTRACTING FOR BEHAVIOR CHANGE AT HOME: DIALOG

Mom and Dad are concerned because Jim, 16, has been coming home later and later from weekend activities. They have decided to talk with Jim.

Dad: "Jim, your Mother and I feel that you are coming home too late on the weekends."

Jim: "What's the matter? Don't you trust me?"

Mom: "That's not the point, Jim. We feel that you are staying out too late and we worry about you. We often don't know when you plan to come home. I don't sleep well until I hear you come in. I guess I need to know everyone is home and safe."

Jim: "What do you want to do? Put a curfew on me?"

Dad: "You know we have tried to let you set your own hours, as long as it didn't make a problem for us. We feel you have been "pushing" that priviledge to the point that it has become a problem for us."

Jim: "How come?"

Dad: "For two reasons: First, when we don't know your plans, we worry about you after 12:00 or 12:30 because sometimes kids need help and we wouldn't even know where to begin if you needed help. We don't want to be alarmists, but there is such a rise in teen violence and crime that your late hours and our concern for your safety add up to worry for us."

Jim: "Oh."

Dad: "The other reason we have a problem with your being out until 1:30 or 2:00 in the morning is that your Mother and I believe that kids shouldn't be out on the streets that late. Many towns set curfews for teenagers around 12:30 to help cut down on the numbers of kids out with very little to do. Some kids who are out that late, drink, drive, look for excitement, and get into touble. We would like to talk about resolving these two problems. Do you have some ideas?"

Jim: "Well, I suppose I can see that you might worry about me. But, really I can take care of myself. You know it's only two years until I'm out on my own. Then what are you going to do?"

Dad: "We will probably always care and sometimes worry about you. It will be different, I think, when you aren't living at home. We will know we can lock up the house when we go to bed. We won't need to include

	your schedule in our plans and we'll know you are an adult with adult responsibilities. That makes a difference in the way some kids and parents think."
Jim:	"So, you want me to tell you what my plans are and come in earlier. Is that it?"
Mom:	"That would help us. How will that work out for you?"
Jim:	"Well, lots of times, my plans change from when I start out an evening or I don't even know what I'm going to be doing until I get together with everyone. What if I gave you a "ball park" estimate on when I'll be home and whatever plans I know before I go? Then, if it changes drastically, I can give you a call?"
Mom:	"That would help our not knowing where you are and when to expect you home. It doesn't solve our belief that you're staying out too late."
Jim:	"I don't see what difference it makes when I get home!"
Dad:	"I can't give you a specific reason except to tell you that Mom and I don't think you should be out so late. I can remember being out really late on a few very special occassions, but not as a usual happening."
Jim:	"Well, when do you think I should be in?"
Mom:	"When do you usually have to have the girls home?"
Jim:	"About midnight."
Mom:	"Then what do you do?"
Jim:	"Me and the guys, we just goof around."
Mom:	"How long does it take you to get home from most of the places you go or from taking a girl home?"
Jim:	"About 15 minutes."
Dad;	"What about another half hour to take friends home and 'goof around'?"
Jim:	"Well....."
Dad:	"That would make it 12:45 when you got home. I think Mom and I could live with that."
Jim:	"What about special occassions?"
Dad:	"We'll take those one at a time as they come up. So - when do we want you to be in by?"

Jim:	"12:45."
Dad:	"Right. And if you do run into any problems with this, you'll call?"
Jim:	"Yeah. I guess I ought to call before it gets to be 12:45, huh?"
Dad:	"That would be a good idea. Let's try this arrangement out for a month (arm on Jim's shoulder) and see how it works out. I'll mark my calendar to check with you in about two weeks to see how it is working for you. OK?"
Jim:	OK."
Dad:	"Then, if you are late and we don't hear from you, we will assume that you need our help - that you might be bleeding to death someplace and that we should call the police to get help to you as quickly as possible. Sometimes, the difference of a few hours can save someone from disaster. Since we know that you are usually quite able to take care of yourself, we will be able to tell the officer, 'We know our son is in trouble because he would have called us if he was going to be out this late.' We will even know where to suggest the police begin looking because we will have some information about where you expected to be. We hope that you never have problems like this but at least we will be in a position to send help and be helpful ourselves."

CONTRACTING FOR BEHAVIOR CHANGE AT SCHOOL: DIALOG.

Teacher:	"For the past few days I have become annoyed several times because you interrupted me while I was talking with another student. (Allow a few seconds so the teen can feel what you're feeling.) I want to be able to discuss your questions with you. Do you suppose we could find another way for you to get my attention instead of your interrupting me all the time?"
Jesse:	"I suppose. But, I have to wait so long to ask my question, I forget what it is."
Teacher:	"So you need to be able to ask your questions before you forget them and I need to continue my conversation with another student without being interrupted?" (Remind Jesse of her personal worth with eye contact and maybe a touch or a smile, if it fits.)
Jesse:	"Yeah."

Teacher:	"I wonder what the possibilities might be?" (BRAINSTORM) "I could try to finish my work with another student faster. What could you do?"
Jesse:	"I don't know."
Teacher:	"Could you write down your question?"
Jesse:	"I guess. Maybe I could ask someone else?"
Teacher:	"That would be fine as long as it doesn't disturb others. Is there anything you can think of that I could do?"
Jesse:	"Well--maybe. You could let me know that you know that I'm waiting. Then I wouldn't have to stand there. I could go sit down."
Teacher:	"OK. That sounds fair. So - we have four ideas. I can hurry with another student. I can give you a signal that I know you're waiting and you....."
Jesse:	"...can ask someone else or write the question down so I won't forget it."
Teacher:	"Can we begin tomorrow?"
Jesse:	"OK."
Teacher:	"Let's give ourselves a week to try these ideas instead of interrupting and then check with each other to see if it's working better for both of us. OK?" (Hand on Jesse's shoulder and a smile.)
Jesse:	"Sure."

ACCORDING TO TEENS, A GOOD PARENT:

Hugs

Listens

Respects

Allows me to make mistakes and grow

Builds self-confidence.

****

"There is no such thing as a NORMAL adolescent.

There are as many different adolescents as there are adolescents!"

ACTIVITY ASSIGNMENT

Go back to the list of "Things Your Teen Does That Bother You" on p. 25. Choose one you think would be appropriate for a contract. Then use the "Planning for Behavior Change" worksheet on p. 114 to prepare for a conversation that would lead up to the contract.

Review the Essentials for Contracting on p. 102. Plan for your conversation with your teen using the upper portion of your "Guide for Observers" worksheet on p. 75. By the next session be prepared to work with a partner to PRACTICE your contracting conversation and then be ready to TRY IT with your teen.

Or, as an alternative assignment:

Look for opportunities to be enCOURAGing with your teen when you might have been disCOURAGing instead. Describe the situation(s).

What did you do?

How did you feel?

How did your teen feel?

READING ASSIGNMENT

HANDBOOK pp. 120-122

"Authority and Rules"
"Learning - Whose Problem?"

Bonus Reading

HANDBOOK pp. 123-126

"Rescuing Kids"
"Kids Need to Own Their Own Feelings"
"The Language of Encouragement"

Tips to Use Tomorrow

HANDBOOK pp. 126-128

"Adults Don't Change"
"Clothes"
"Winners" by Denis Waitley

AUTHORITY AND RULES

The principal source of authority in families, schools, organizations, and governments is the consent to be governed. Authority is directly linked to rules and people who are given the right to tell others what to do. The benefits and costs of this authority become evident as it is exercised. Security, fairness, protection, and efficiency are a few. However, authority, when misused or perceived to be misused, can generate resistance, rebellion, and general destruction of order.

We see the results of disorder not only in national revolts and guerrilla warfare, but in families. Much as we would like to believe otherwise, WE CAN'T MAKE PEOPLE DO WHAT THEY CHOOSE NOT TO DO!

When do we have the right to tell others what to do? How do we get others to cooperate?

In families and in schools adults are given authority over students and children. Power, privilege, and responsibility come with authority.

ACTIVITY: Discuss the issue of **authority** with your class or family using these steps:

1. Think back 24 hours and make a list of the times some authority has had an impact on you.

2. What would happen if there was permissiveness rather than authority in your community? At school? At work? At home?

3. What characterizes well-used authority? Allows input from the governed? Delegates some of its power?

4. What happens in schools or families or to you personally when authority is misused?

During the discussion of authority, rules will probably be mentioned. Rules tell the governed what Authority expects.

"Don't fight in the halls or on the playground."

"Don't throw food in the cafeteria."

"Don't leave the school or playground without permission."

"Absolutely no talking on the way to PE or Music classes."

Some RULES about rules:

They should be:

1. OF, BY, and FOR the people who have to live with them. (The basic premise of our Constitution.)

2. Designed to achieve a purpose.

3. Simply stated.

4. Clear about what is expected: What behavior *to do* vs. what *not* do.

5. Possible to follow.

6. Designed to minimize infringement on important personal values. (The individual's dignity remains intact.)

7. Fair.

8. As few as possible.

Always check the validity of rules by asking:

Is this rule necessary? Or is there a better way to achieve my purpose?

ACTIVITY:

List three of your rules. Evaluate them using the criteria in RULES about Rules.

1.

2.

3.

Note any changes you might make to improve (or eliminate) them.

LEARNING - WHOSE PROBLEM?

Is it the teacher's job to teach kids? Or is it the teacher's job to **provide opportunities to learn?**

Is s/he to make kids learn or provide ways for kids **to decide to learn?**

What if parents and teachers decided to let all resistant students **decide to learn?**

EXAMPLE:

Dan is a fifth grade student who decided to quit learning in the second grade. He has been tested and is neither emotionally disturbed nor retarded. However, he is about to be placed in a self-contained special education room because his teachers have tried everything and "don't know what else to do with him."

For three years, Dan has not only received a lot of attention for not learning but has been able to control the feelings and behavior of the adults around him.

What would happen if he were allowed to decide about learning with no further coersion from adults? What if his fifth grade teacher told him she would be happy to provide opportunities for him to learn when he's ready? But that he would have to let her know by telling her so.

Until he's ready, he can sit in the back of the fifth grade room. That is, if he doesn't disturb the other students. If he is disruptive the teacher will find another place in the building where he can wait until he decides he wants to learn and where he won't disturb others' learning.

As a well-practiced, resistant kid, Dan will probably sit for several weeks, maybe months. However, he has been sitting for several years already. Once he decides he wants to learn, he will also probably have to catch up on a lot of work from second, third, and fourth grades. However, smart kids who really want to learn can do this in less than a year.

Obviously this approach won't work without parent support. Both the parents and Dan will need to be part of conferences when "turning the learning problem back to Dan" is discussed. Teachers and parents will have to "hang in there" while he tests their resolve. The trouble with most of the things that we try with kids is that we don't try them for long enough!

During the past decade, teachers have been trying to teach all kids. However, because teaching can only occur when people **want to learn,** this expectation is unrealistic. Providing an environment in which learning can occur is the part of the learning cycle that teachers control - and interestingly enough, a lot of what this course is all about. Kids **decide to learn.**

RESCUING KIDS

When we rescue kids, we are telling them they can't handle the situation. Discouraged kids get into trouble. So when solving problems we want to build kids' self-esteem, particularly in the area of seeing themselves as capable people who influence their world.

Hurting inside leads to change in what and how we do things.

"People change their behavior when they're hurting." Or so it's been said for centuries. Embarrassment, deprivation, spankings, stocks, prison, tortures are all punishment imposed from the outside. If they were effective most of the world's problems would have been solved by now.

So the statement needs to be expanded to say: **People change their behavior when they're hurting and they know they are the cause.** They can't escape by blaming someone else.

Troy worked all summer long at a construction job to earn enough money to buy a car when he turned 16. He saved his money and opened a bank account. Then he discovered how easy it was to withdraw the money. $20 here, $40 there - a movie, gas for his buddy's car, etc. At the beginning of the summer he thought he would have $1,000 for a car. By September, "Well, maybe a $500 car would do." By the time his November birthday rolled around, he didn't even have that much. Bummer!

What if we had given Troy a few thoughtful reminders: "If you hadn't spent your money on ---, you would have your car!" Or "encouragement" throughout the summer, "If you don't quit spending so much money on ---, you won't be able to buy your car." What if we had said, "I told you so!"

Lesson lost! The hurt would have been imposed from the outside! Troy would have had an escape valve - someone to blame. He could have been angry at us for letting him know he couldn't handle the situation.

Problems are best solved by their owners. Left to suffer some of the smaller hurts in life, kids learn and their destructive behaviors change before they become life threatening. A child not rescued may be a child saved.

KIDS NEED TO OWN THEIR OWN FEELINGS -- AND THEIR OWN LEARNING!

Kids need to feel that their learning is more important to them than it is to anyone else. Catch kids doing well and say, "I'll bet you feel good about that." When we feel good about things we can say, "Well, I finally finished grading all those papers. I'm all caught up and I really feel good about that." Or: "Boy, my car looks so great now that it's all cleaned up. I'll feel really good when I pick up my rider tomorrow!"

Kids copy adults. Give them something positive to copy. It's rather ironic that we seldom give kids something to model that might encourage finishing school work or enjoying learning. And yet, that's a major part of kids' "work" in growing up.

We need to:

1. Let kids own their own feelings.
2. Model our feelings about things we do.
3. Let kids know how deeply we are invested in experiencing those activities in which we learn - namely school, reading, etc.

If you're wondering who owns the worry about doing well in school, you might ask, "Who worries most about whether or not s/he does his or her work?" Who worries about grades?"

It is interesting to note that one of the groups who have the biggest trouble with their teens about academics in school is parents who are classroom teachers or university professors. Professors tend to make academics so important that their teens know who will take most of the units of worry about school. If the teens are rebellious, they also know just which button to push to set their parents off on a tirade. Do poorly in school!

Teachers who make students' learning so important to the teacher set them up to let teachers worry about it. In fact, some students only feel good at school when they have the adults hooked into a power struggle over their learning. Then they feel empowered instead of their usual feelings of impotence at school. Each time we try to **make** kids learn, do the work, or be neat, we set them up to resist.

What if we said to teens, "Don't sweat it. We offer seventh grade every year?" Then who might worry? That is, if they really believe that seventh grade could come around again for them next year.

Schools have to involve parents in this kind of an approach, explaining that the more we push, the more their teens seem to resist. Parents and teens need to believe that this is a situation where the teen's learning is important to him or her **first.**

Many times we set things up with teens by telling them something "is good for them".

"Eat your breakfast so you won't get hungry."

"Don't stay out late because you might get into trouble."

"Clean off your desk so you can get organized."

And the kid can say,

"I won't get hungry."

"I won't get into trouble."

"I am already as organized as I want to be."

They can argue with you.

Another way to say these things so kids can accept them and go along with more of our suggestions is to say:

"Eat your breakfast so I won't worry about your missing a meal."

"Don't stay out too late so I won't have to worry about you." (You need to be careful there - what is too late? Agree on a time, after which you will probably worry. This is not designed to send the message to a teen that they turn into a pumpkin and can't take care of themselves after a certain hour. It will simply take care of adults who care and worry when kids are late. I worry about my spouse when he is unusually late, too, unless he calls to alleviate my concern.)

"I am better organized when my desk is cleared. You may want to try it." Your teen still has a choice!

When we can own our own feelings about things and let teens own their own feelings and the responsibility for things that happen in their lives, worry and the possibility for argument will diminish.

THE LANGUAGE OF ENCOURAGEMENT

Some years ago, several adults went into business together. Obviously, they all wanted to "help" the business move along successfully. So when things didn't go as they had all hoped, they would offer "suggestions". The problem was that some members of the group felt they were not trusted to do "their" part of the job of making the business successful. They were always looking over each others' shoulders offering advice and "being helpful". The business did not survive these attempts to be "encouraging".

We do the same things to kids. Our constant surveillance leaves teens feeling mistrusted and incapable of controlling their own world.

So how can we be encouraging to teens?

Don Dinkmeyer suggests:

1. Give teens responsibility and once given, it becomes theirs. Provide help only when it is requested.

2. Let teens learn from the logic of the consequence. Dialog, when they want to talk, will prove helpful. From dialog comes judgement for future actions.

3. Appreciate their contributions. Teens often feel that things they do well aren't recognized. Adults feel that way, too. We begin to feel that doing well is an **assumed attribute** and doesn't need recognition.

EXAMPLE:

I overheard a Principal talking with a colleague one day. "She doesn't need encouragement. She's such a self-starter!"

I think that was a compliment. Unfortunately, we *all* need encouragement through recognition of a job well done!

4. Ask teens for their opinions and suggestions. That's one way we feel respected and genuinely needed. Most of us learn best when we are involved in a meaningful way in that learning.

5. Encourage participation in decision making. All of us are more likely to comply with decisions we have helped make.

How hard would you work on this course if it had been a compulsory one?

6. Don't catastrophize mistakes. If asked, use Dialog to determine what different actions might be taken another time. Then assume the same mistake won't be made again.

7. Focus on efforts. With the strong emphasis on improving academic achievement, we are in danger of discouraging learners. I hear words such as "more", "harder", and "perfect". The road to excellence is made up of effort, mistakes, improvement, and finally learning or skill. It is most encouraging to know our efforts are recognized and supported. To do our best may be better than to do it perfectly.

8. Turn liabilities into assets. There are many books available today on positive thinking. A common theme is viewing a problem as an opportunity.

9. Show confidence in your teen's decisions.

TIPS TO USE TOMORROW

We need to develop the courage to be imperfect. Most of us won't share our good ideas until we are sure they are free of errors. As a result, we deprive each other of lots of assistance and encouragement.

One solution is to write DRAFT on things we produce. Then we can share and always say, if we discover an error, "Well, it's only a draft, you know."

ADULTS DON'T CHANGE

I asked more than 250 teenagers in three very different High Schools, if they thought adults could change. More than 85 percent of them said "No". Many of them said "Oh, they try. But they're so set in their ways!"

When I shared this information with adults, comments included, "I think adults can change, but it takes a lot of effort." We have to practice doing something differently for a long time to have it truly "second" nature.

We decide to practice new approaches only after some other crucial decisions have been made. Change begins with:

I realize I **need** to change.

I decide I **want** to change.

I discover I **can** change.

I decide I **will** change.

I **plan the action** I am going to take.

Then, I **practice** and expect mistakes, correcting until.....

I am **skilled** (it is easy) at doing it a new way.

Some will move from step to step fairly quickly. Others will move slowly, stopping and starting, encouraged and discouraged, going forward two steps and back one.

CLOTHES

Assorted thoughts about CLOTHES:

Kids are old enough to choose their own clothes by second grade.

It is reasonable to expect dirty laundry to be in the hamper.

Children, ages 5 to 6, can sort laundry. Children, ages 6 to 8, can run the washer. By 10 or 11 they can add bleach. And by 12 they can mend. School age children can fold laundry and put it away.

Teens are ready for: "You wear it. You wash it."

Teach the use of the washer and dryer; how to measure soap, remove stains, etc. For teens who walk out of their clothes and leave them, a "personal" laundry basket sometimes helps.

Wearing "strange" clothes is your problem only when they are going someplace with you.

What about kids who don't take care of or lose their clothes? The rule in our house is: "I buy the first one."

WINNERS

"Practice optimism and positive expectancy. It's contagious!"
"Winners dwell on their desire, not their limitations."

- Denis Waitley -

— NOTES —

MODULE VII
PLAYING THE SCHOOL GAME

WAYS TO PLAY THE GAMES OF LIFE

1. Decide to play **better than others.**

2. Decide **not to play** at all.

3. Decide to play **antigame.**

4. Decide to **change the game.**

5. Decide to **mimic the game.**

6. Decide to **create your own game.**

EXAMPLES of "ways to play the game".
(Write in your own examples or those of the group.)

TRANSITIONS IN SCHOOLS

1930

—14 children per classroom - all ages.

—Older children teaching younger children with the teacher checking for understanding. Many teachers in one classroom.

—Very little opportunity for group assignment so many individual ones with the teacher checking for:

What is SIGNIFICANT?
Why is it SIGNIFICANT?
HOW can it be APPLIED
   to other situations?

DIALOG, which leads to WISDOM
   and JUDGEMENT.

—Students learn through designing lessons for others and teaching them and Dialog with the teacher. Two way verbal communication.

—Assessment of achievement and growth primarily through verbal dialog and applied problem solving. Older -younger and Student -Teacher.

TODAY

—At least 25-30 children per classroom.

—Homogenous groups, no older and younger children to teach each other. One teacher with no time or set pattern to check for understanding except by test.

—Group assignments and lessons because of common age, time limits, and the assumption that because we design curriculum to fit certain ages and growth patterns, all in a homogenous class will be ready at about the same time.

Too many students to have time for DIALOG with each regularly to check for understanding so do it with paper/pencil testing.

—Students learn through listening and reading. One way paper/pencil (primarily) communication.

—Assessment of achievement and growth primarily through reading and writing on questions of the knowledge and information level of thinking. Very little practical application.

TEACHING/LEARNING MODELS

ACTIVITY ASSIGNMENT

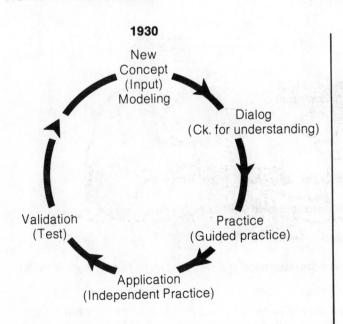

1930

New Concept (Input) Modeling

Dialog (Ck. for understanding)

Practice (Guided practice)

Application (Independent Practice)

Validatioh (Test)

Today

Concept — Explanation — Concept
Explanation — Test

51% of the population
does not learn well-this way.

ACTIVITY ASSIGNMENT:

Using the materials you have been practicing, set up a contract for behavior change with your teen. Be prepared to discuss its results at the next session.

Alternative Assignment:

Find out how your school and/or some of your child's teachers approach "teaching" new ideas. How might you contribute to your school's efforts to teach your teen? Be prepared to talk about this next session.

Alternative Assignment:

Write a letter to yourself. Pick four ideas you have learned about in this program that you want to try at school or at home. Indicate how you think using each idea will improve your teaching, parenting, or your relationship with your teen. Give this letter to your leader in a self-addressed, stamped envelope to be mailed to you in two months. This assignment will help you follow up on some of the good intentions you have now.

READING ASSIGNMENT

HANDBOOK pp. 132-136

"Steps to Problem Solving"

Bonus Reading

HANDBOOK pp. 136-139

"You Really Oughta Wanna"
"Which TAKE do You Test?" by Ed Frierson
"Normal Distribution Curve 'itis'"

Tips to Use Tomorrow

HANDBOOK pp. 139-140

"Additional Thoughts on Time Out"
"Additional Thoughts on Contracting"
"Skipping School"

STEPS TO PROBLEM SOLVING

To solve problems and make decisions, learn to:

1. Analyze problems and **understand** their complexities.

2. Develop the **judgement** to make wise decisions.

3. Develop the ability to communicate in a way that allows us to work with others.

We all need these skills if we are to become and continue to be capable, happy adults. Problems are a part of life. Someone forgets to feed the family pet. Three people want to watch two different TV programs on one TV set. The custodian continually forgets to unlock the classroom door in the morning. Students are forever missing their homework assignment. The car won't start because someone let the battery run down. We need to develop skills to deal with these problems, if for no other reason than to lower the stress in our daily lives.

Teens also need to learn to deal with the stresses and conflicts in their lives. There's too much homework to do in one evening. A big date is coming up and there's no gas money. A friend didn't do what he said he would do.

Parents and teachers need to teach problem solving and decision making skills to their teens. One of the ways to do this is to include children in the problem solving and decision making process as early and as often as possible. One of the key elements in this process is common sense!

Problems may be approached in at least two ways:

1. We can just wait until a problem comes along and then:

      —Decide to deal with it.
      —Decide to ignore it. It may go away!

2. We can anticipate problems and then:

      —Decide on a plan that may eliminate or neutralize the problem.
      —Decide to ignore the problem. It may go away!

In both cases, when we think there is a possibility the problem may go away, doing nothing may be the best way to handle it. Sometimes, we anticipate and worry about situations that either never happen, or work themselves out in time. In those instances, we can make the problem worse by getting involved. This is particularly true if the problem isn't ours to begin with!

EXAMPLE:

      For the past month, there has been a "metal on metal" rattle under the hood of the truck Troy and Scott drive back and forth to school.

      Dad has two choices: Let the boys find out what happens when they do not keep the car in repair

OR

      Get involved and fix it, either quietly or with much fuss about how the boys ought to be taking care of their "means of transportation".

      In this case, since no one else drives the truck but the boys, this problem is best left to them.

Whether adults are solving problems and making decisions for themselves or are involved in teaching teens the process here are some steps which can lead to success:

Clarify the problem (as You see it)

1. Describe the problem - what do you think the problem is?

2. How do you feel about the problem and what are your expectations?

3. Think about how your teen might view the problem and how s/he might feel about it (if the problem involves your teen).

4. Decide what you would like to have happen based upon your thinking in 1-3 above. What behaviors would you like? What outcomes can you plan for?

When problem solving with children, be careful to describe behaviors in **observable** terms.

Clarifying the problem helps you decide what your GOALS are.

Decide what to do - Brainstorm alternatives

Teens need a lot of practice doing this. They have difficulty generating alternatives.

Ed Frierson suggested earlier that one of the ways we can deal with problems is to...

A. Look at the **environment**

. . . think of possiblities for changing the environment to either solve the problem or cause the teen to look at the problem in a different way. Ed suggested that when clothes on the floor are driving us crazy, we might just "hang the pants on the light". Earlier in this book we suggested that notes "from the plant" needing water or "from the dirty dishes in the sink" might cause teens to see their environment and the problems caused in a different way.

Suppose you have a child whose study habits are really poor. Maybe the environment for study is not encouraging organization and undisturbed attention. Changes in that environment might encourage better study habits.

Parents who want their kids to hang up their coats can use convenient hooks to encourage this behavior. Schools that want to encourage teens to take care of the facilities can provide the students with opportunities to decorate the halls and classrooms, the lockers, and "common" areas.

Another approach to deciding what to do involves:

B. Taking the time for you and your teen to think through the problem together before it happens and **head it off**.

Think about the problem. Clarify it in your mind. Decide what the GOALS should be. Use brainstorming to come up with as many alternatives as you can for "heading off the problem". Check out the consequences for each idea.

EXAMPLE:

IDEA	CONSEQUENCE
Sally takes her Final Exam tomorrow.	She will probably flunk, as she is unprepared.
Sally stays up all night and studies.	She may or may not be alert enough to do well on the Final.
Sally talks to the teacher and tries to reschedule the Final.	The teacher may or may not go along with the idea. If she does, she can do much better on the Final.
Sally could skip school today and study.	She may or may not get away with it.

Planning to head off a problem should include specifics about the "what" of our expectations but also, the "when".

C. Planning alternatives

This is another way to look at problems and make decisions. If two sisters are always fighting over "whose blouse do you have on?", planning for alternatives to help the two girls "keep track" of their own things can cut down on the fighting considerably.

Clean rooms are a problem in many homes. How many alternative solutions might you and your teen come up with for solving that problem?

Pin-ups on the locker doors sometimes cause a problem in schools. What alternatives might there be to eliminating "decorating" lockers completely? Maybe the "pin-ups" have to be INSIDE, not outside the doors.

Fighting on family vacations is often a result of boredom during a long ride. What alternatives can you plan as a family to "head off" the problem?

Once you have come up with ideas about what to do, then,

Choose the best option

...and figure out the steps for implementing it.

Who is responsible?
When will it be done?
How will it get done?
Where will it be done?

Follow that closely with...

Carrying out your decision

with firmness, dignity, and respect!

And the final step for adults . . .

Acknowledge efforts in the right direction!

Throughout the **You've Got To Be Kid-ding** program, you have been learning a variety of skills that you can use in the Problem Solving and Decision Making process. Remember to use them as you work with your teens.

1. "I" Messages.

2. Good Listening.

3. Acknowledging feelings.

4. Encouragement.

5. Logical Consequences.

6. Rules (as a last resort).

7. Dialog.

8. Goal Setting.

9. Brainstorming.

10. Common Sense.

11. Think Time.

12. Humor.

BONUS READING

YOU REALLY OUGHTA WANNA!

Not only do we expect teens to do things the way we want them done, but we often expect them to **want** to do things the way we want them done.

"Kids ought to want to do homework."
"They should want to help out around the house."

Teens do or don't do things for lots of reasons. (The same is true for adults.) When teens aren't doing what we expect, before we ask ourselves, "What can I do to change this?" we should ask, "Why do I feel this should be changed?" Once we're really sure the situation needs to be changed, we should try and determine if the problem is "can't" or "won't".

If the problem is "can't", we may need to clarify our expectations or do some teaching so that next time the job will be performed more to our liking.

If the problem is "won't", looking for the reason may yield a clue to the solution.

EXAMPLES:

Sometimes good performance brings penalties. "If I make good grades, my friends will think I'm an egghead." "When I tell my Dad how I really feel, he cuts me down."

Sometimes bad performance is rewarded. "I know I shouldn't drink, but when I do, at least my Mother pays attention to me!"

If we don't know if the problem is a "can't" or a "won't", we can:

1. Ask the teen, or
2. Ask ourselves, "Could s/he do this if s/he absolutely had to?"

There's a good rule to remember: If you want someone to do something in a particular way, **make it matter to that person.** As with flowers, water the performance you want, and watch it grow!

WHICH <u>TAKE</u> DO YOU WANT TO <u>TEST</u>?   Ed Frierson

Student participation in evaluation

As alternatives in education become more numerous, schools experiment with many approaches to evaluation and grading. However, the idea of alternatives in testing is still a one-way street. The teacher is the one who designs and provides the alternatives.

When a teacher has several tests over the same material, she may ask, "Which test do you want to take?" No matter which test the student chooses, it remains the teacher's test and the grading will be a one-way judgement.

From the world of radios, movies, and TV here's a new idea. It might be called "the screen test" or the "make a tape" approach to evaluation. The key element is that the student decides how best to convince the teacher that he is prepared, that he has learned, and that he has passed.

Students may be paired so that one is the "star" while the other one is the "agent". The agent is going to sell his star to the teacher (the producer).

First, the agent finds out what the producer thinks is important. What qualities, characteristics, or performance behaviors are desirable? The producer should be looking for certain special traits which can be described to the agent.

Next, the agent tries to get his star ready to impress the producer. In the movie world the agent would get several film clips together which show his star actually on the silver screen. Screen tests are made when a producer looks at one or several short films (sometimes referred to as "takes") and decides if the actor has the qualities which he is seeking for a feature picture.

The agent wants his star to look good! He hopes to convince the producer that his star is ready for the big picture. He proves that his star is just what the producer needs. The agent and star select the best evidence thay have to give to the producer.

Do you see how this could work in the classroom? The kids would prepare to convince the teacher that they had learned the material. They might make several approaches (a skit, some paper work, a panel, etc.) and then the kids would decide which "take" (activity) they would like the teacher to "test" (evaluate for learning).

A variation of "which take do you test" is the radio approach. In radio work, personalities looking for new positions or being evaluated are asked to "make a tape". This tape is a live, on-the-air performance which demonstrates the disc jockey or newscaster's abilities. Of course, he may submit any tape he wishes for evaluation.

Using a tape recorder, students might "make a tape" to be evaluated by a committee. Tapes should be original and non-restrictive. When a student believes one of his tapes will convince a committee that he has learned something, he submits his favorite tape for testing. The student, not the teacher, decides "which take do you test?"

NORMAL DISTRIBUTION CURVE "ITIS"

In our schools we have established the idea of the "normal distribution curve". The middle group of kids have "C" skills. The best ones "A"s and the worst ones "D"s. It is frowned upon for a whole class to get "A"s just as it is for all to get "D"s and "F"s.

The age-old conflict of how to "grade" performance is directly contrary to all we know about motivation and encouragement for people. Human relations experts tell us over and over again, "People become what they think we think they can!" How might we get the message across to our teenagers that each and everyone of them is a potential **winner?**

1. Be very clear about our goals and expectations for their development and learning.

2. Involve the teen in the development of **their** goals and expectations.

3. Provide specific **feedback** as soon as possible. A question we should ask first, before we give our feedback is, "What did you think I asked you to do?" Then we can be very specific about how to get closer to the mark the next time.

4. Give specific information about how we feel about the job as it was done. If we feel good, let them know. If we're upset, let them know. Remember: the feelings are about the task -NOT THE PERSON!

5. Look them square in the eye - touch them in some way - and let them know you're honestly on their side. It's amazing the number of teens that I've talked with who believe adults are out to get them - to trick them so they can play, "I got'cha!"

6. Let them know how much you value them - that your feelings about their performance are not the same as your feelings about them.

Have you ever seen a football coach out on the field yelling, shaking his fist at a player who is hustling off the field, having just fumbled the ball - really getting a "chewing out" and after it's over, and the player has a minute to think about it, getting a slap on the rear or a right to the shoulder as the player turns to go to the line or back out on the field? Great coaches love their players and every member of the team knows it.

7. THEN IT'S OVER! No more comments, last words, or reminders. Let's grow **winners** and forget the normal distribution curve!

TIPS TO USE TOMORROW

ADDITIONAL THOUGHTS ON TIME OUT

1. It is not a punishment. It is a way for adults to take care of themselves when kids decide to be obnoxious.

2. It is administered in a cool, calm, collected, and prompt manner. Kids do not have to like going. They simply have to go.

3. It should provide bland versus negative attention. It might even be boring.

4. It can work for one child who is misbehaving or a group which is misbehaving. The spot needs to be a different one for each in the group.

5. It works best from age three to twelve. At the high school level, it can be used but must be done with care.

ADDITIONAL THOUGHTS ON CONTRACTING:

Contracts are commitments by BOTH sides. Remember, kids are not really sure adults will stick to their half of the bargain.

Contracts are best when they are written down.

Contracts are agreements to "do something" not to "not do something".

Contracts are fair.

Contracts are designed to be successful.

Contracts are to be negotiated - a skill teens can learn.

It's OK for the teen to grumble and gripe. We do a lot of things we don't want to do and we don't often do them cheerfully.

Contracts which add and subtract points should be avoided.

The payoff of a contract should come **after** the performance and as soon as possible.

****

Question: Is there one unsolved problem within your sphere of interests or responsibilities? Let your teens watch you struggle for a solution. Let them experience you as a **learner.**

SKIPPING SCHOOL

What is a good consequence for SKIPPING SCHOOL? Certainly not Out-Of-School suspension! Many schools use supervised In-School suspension which not only allows schools to control the environment but encourages students to catch up on missed work.

MODULE VIII
FILLING TEEN'S TOOLBOX FOR LIFE

CREATIVE PROBLEM SOLVING SKILLS

1. Fluency - How many ideas can you generate about something?

2. Flexibility - How many ways can you look at the same idea?

3. Originality - Anything that does not happen very often.

4. Elaboration - Twisting, turning, reshaping, or revisualizing an idea as you think about it.

Creativity is a Style, a Perspective, a Way of Looking at Things.

One of the keys to Happiness in Life is to deal with problems in an expansive way -generating lots of ideas no matter how far fetched, searching those ideas for the unusual, the original, and then, **risking** a "go for it" attitude!

BRAINSTORMING

Rules for Brainstorming:

1. No criticism or judgement of ideas is permitted.

2. Free-wheeling is encouraged; the more original or unusual the idea, the better.

3. Quantity, not quality, is the objective.

4. Piggybacking ideas is desirable.

M-I-N-D S-T-R-E-T-C-H-I-N-G Q-U-E-S-T-I-O-N-S

1. Think up ten practical uses for pop tops.

2. How many different ways can you use a frisbee?

3. Think of other ways than national boundries to organize life on earth.

4. Create an idea about something. Then:

Make it small.
Make it lighter.
Add color.
Change its shape.
Change its meaning.
Combine two ideas into one.
Substitute other places.
Reverse it.
Add time.
Exaggerate it.
Make some parts bigger.
Take away parts.

EXPLORING ALTERNATIVES WITH TEENS

Use Questions:

1. If your friend had this problem, what would you tell him or her?

2 Will any of those ideas work for you?

3. If you were a Mom, how would you deal with this problem?

4. If you went to your friend for advice what might he or she suggest?

5. Propose alternatives and their consequences with equal "pizzaz". (i.e., Wearing a coat or not wearing one on a cold day. Getting the homework done or not getting it done. By giving equal "pizzaz" to the alternatives, we truly allow teens to **choose their own solutions.)**

(Be sure, when you are working with your teen and giving equal "pizzaz" to all of the alternatives, that, if they choose a poor one, you can live with the results. If you know you cannot, let the teen know that that choice would be hard for you to live with.)

WAYS TO WIN!

CHECKING	vs.	Assuming
EXPLORING	vs.	Taking Care of Things
ENCOURAGING	vs.	Directing and Supervising
CELEBRATING	vs.	Expecting
RESPECTING and DIALOG	vs.	Adultisms

PERCEPTIONS AND SKILLS

We have discussed seven basic perceptions and skills which are necessary for young people to possess if they are to be successful, capable, and independent people. You were introduced to them early in this program. We will list them again for your review.

Three perceptions

1. I am **capable.**

2. I **contribute** in meaningful ways and I am **genuinely needed.**

3. I can **influence** what happens to me.

Four skills

1. Strong **intrapersonal** skills.

2. Strong **interpersonal** skills.

3. Strong **situational** skills.

4. Good **judgmental** skills.

TO TEACH THE TOOLS FOR LIFE TO ADOLESCENTS

We must:

1. Understand the tools.

2. See progress in very small increments.

3. Resist ramming things through.

4. Be more mature than the child.

In what shape are the tools in your toolbox ?

Get out your toolbox. Polish up your tools. Then check with your teens for any teaching or polishing they may need to do on their tools. Being a parent or a teacher carries with it the joys of watching the fruits of your work and the pain of watching our young struggle and grow. As you put the many thoughts and ideas from **You've Got To Be Kid-ding** into practice, remember, **becoming excellent** takes time, patience, effort, practice, and a sense of humor. Enjoy these teen years. Ease the stresses of being a teacher or a parent. Help make being a teen more fun. Keep in mind, **You've Got To Be Kid-ding** each and every day. Your children's future depends on it!

You don't have to be good to start . . . but . . . you have to start...to be good!

NEVERENDING EFFORT

Wouldn't it be nice if once we had a good thing going with our teens, it would just continue on its own? Unfortunately, frequent care and feeding are necessary for any relationship. Teens need to learn that they too must continue to earn the support of adults in their lives by working in their own self interest and by being considerate of those around them. If they learn this lesson well, it will stand them in good stead in their relationships with others, on their jobs, and in the new homes they create with their mates and children.

TIPS TO USE TOMORROW

The Creative Teaching Style ... A Way of Looking at Things

School Learning

	CONTENT	APPROACH	ATTITUDE
F L	What are *all* the sources of information ideas and problems that I can find?	What are *all* of the ways of spending time in school other than readin', 'ritin', & 'rithmetic?	What are *all* of the moods and attitudes that I can be aware of at any one time?
F X	What are the most remote, least likely and obscure materials that I can use?	When and how is the most unlikely, unpredictable and unreasonable time and process?	What shifts of attention can I use to provide unlikely pairings of feelings & emotions?
O	What subjects, areas of study can I introduce that no one else has *ever* thought of?	How can I go about introducing a subject or activity that no one has *ever* suggested?	How can I bring about a change of attitude that no one else may *ever* have had before?
E	What twists, turns and nuances of facts, theories and subjects can I introduce?	How can I give feedback to help a student, discover a more unusual or interesting way of doing it?	How often can I go beyond my first reaction and enjoy a wide range of attitudes toward experience?

(THE CREATIVE STYLE — left margin label)

Fluency	The **number of things one thinks about.**
Flexibility	A **shift in the things one thinks about.**
Originality	The **uniqueness of the things one thinks about.**
Elaboration	The **transformation of the things one thinks about.**

There's a Ping-Pong ball in a hole. The hole is a little bit bigger than the ball. It's longer than your arm. Or anyone else's arm. There are no sticks around. What can you do to get the ball out of the hole?

SOME CALL IT A "HIGHER LEVEL OF LOVE"

Actively wanting and encouraging your teen's unique decision-making and problem solving ability.

Enjoying watching your teen decide, make mistakes, and grow.

Developing positive thoughts and beliefs about the capabilities of your teen.

Allowing your teen the dignity of experiencing the results of his or her decisions with firmness and respect.

POSTPROGRAM QUESTIONNAIRE

This questionnaire will give you a measure of your growth from the beginning to the end of your sessions in **YOU'VE GOT TO BE KID-DING!** Mark your level of comfort or skill with an X. Connect the Xs with lines to create your profile. Compare this profile with the results of your questionnaire on p. xii.

DESIRED SKILLS	PRESENT LEVEL OF COMPETENCE					
	Inadequate —			Adequate +		
I can list at least five changes in the way families operated from 1930 to the present.	3	2	1	1	2	3
I can list at least five characteristics of a family or school environment that lead to the development of capable young people.	3	2	1	1	2	3
I know how to identify "who owns a problem" and how to leave the problem with its "owner".	3	2	1	1	2	3
I know how to teach children Responsibility, Self-control, and Self-discipline.	3	2	1	1	2	3
I know and understand the elements necessary for adolescents to feel Capable.	3	2	1	1	2	3
I am comfortable with my methods for establishing a learning environment in my classroom.	3	2	1	1	2	3
I know and use methods for disciplining teens that encourage motivation, cooperation, and achievement.	3	2	1	1	2	3
I communicate my classroom needs and feelings effectively to my students.	3	2	1	1	2	3
I feel I use good listening skills when talking with teens.	3	2	1	1	2	3
I understand the difference between the learning outcomes of punishment and natural or logical consequences.	3	2	1	1	2	3
I feel that I use effective consequences that maintain firmness, dignity, and respect for myself and teens.	3	2	1	1	2	3
I feel that I use effective methods of encouragement with adolescents.	3	2	1	1	2	3
I know the elements necessary to give Meaning, Purpose, and Significance in people's lives.	3	2	1	1	2	3
I understand the effects of self-esteem on adolescent behavior.	3	2	1	1	2	3
I create a learning environment where self-esteem is nurtured.	3	2	1	1	2	3

I understand the elements of an effective behavioral contract and can apply them.   3   2   1   1   2   3

My approach to teaching is effective in producing learners who achieve well within their individual limits and feel capable.   3   2   1   1   2   3

I understand ideas teens have about their lives, goals, priorities, and experiences from their point of viewing.   3   2   1   1   2   3

I can teach adolescents to be effective decision makers and problem solvers.   3   2   1   1   2   3

I know and understand the perceptions teens must have about themselves in order to function well as adults.   3   2   1   1   2   3

I know and understand the basic skills people must have in order to function effectively in a democratic system.   3   2   1   1   2   3

I understand the elements and importance of Dialog and can use it effectively.   3   2   1   1   2   3

— NOTES —

References for Further Reading and Practice

Books:

Bayard, Robert T. and Bayard, Jean. *How To Deal With Your Acting-up Teenager.* New York: M. Evans Co., 1983.

Becker, Wesley C. *Parents Are Teachers.* Champaign, IL: Research Press, 1974.

Blanchard, Kenneth H. and Hersey, Paul. *The Family Game.* Reading, MA: Addison Wesley, 1978.

Blanchard, Kenneth and Johnson, Spencer. *The One Minute Manager.* New York: William Morrow, 1982.

Buntman, Peter H. land Saris, Eleanor M. *How to Live With Your Teenager.* New York: Bantom Books, 1983.

Cline, Foster W. *Parent Education Text.* Evergreen, CO: Evergreen Consultants, 1982.

D'Augelli, Judith and Weener, Joan. *Communication and Parenting Skills.* University Park, PA: National Institute on Drug Abuse, USDA, 1979.

Davitz, Lois and Davitz, Joel. *How To Live Almost Happily With a Teenager.* Winston Press, 1982.

Dinkmeyer, Don and Losoncy, Lewis. *The Encouragement Book.* Englewood Cliffs, NJ, 1980.

Dodson, Fitzhugh. *How To Discipline With Love.* New York: New American Library, 1977.

Faber, Adele and Mazlish, Elaine. *How To Talk With Kids So They'll Listen And How To Listen So They'll Talk.* New York: Editorial Correspondents, 1980.

Faber, Adele and Mazlish, Elaine. *Liberated Parents: Liberated Children.* New York: Avon Books, 1975.

Fay, James M. *Discipline With Dignity.* Foxton, CO: School Consultant Services, 1981.

Ginot, Haim. *Between Parent And Teenager.* New York: Avon Books, 1969.

Glenn, H. Stephen and Warner, Joel W. *Developing Capable Young People.* Hurst, TX, 1982.

Gordon, Thomas. *Parent Effectiveness Training and Teacher Effectiveness Training.* New York: Peter H. Wyden, Inc., 1970.

Losoncy, Lewis. *Turning People On: How To Be An Encouraging Person.* Englewood Cliffs, NJ: New York: Prentice-Hall, 1977.

Losoncy, Lewis. *You Can Do It: How To Encourage Yourself.* Englewood Cliffs, NJ: Prentice-Hall, 1980.

Mager, Robert F. *Analyzing Performance Problems.* Belmont, CA: Fearon Pitman, 1970.

Nelson, Jane. *Positive Discipline.* Fair Oaks, CA: Adlerian Counseling Center, 1981.

Nicholson, Luree and Torbet, Laura. *How To Fight Fair With Your Kids...And Win!* New York: Harcourt Brace, 1980.

Perls, Frederick S. *In And Out Of The Garbage Pail.* New York: Bantom Books, 1972.

Spellman, Chas. and Williams, Rachel. *Pitching In.* Rolling Hills Estates, CA: Jalmar Press, 1981.

Walton, Francis W. *Winning Teenagers Over in Home and School.* Chicago: Practical Psychology Assoc., 1980.

Wells, Joel. *How To Survive With Your Teen-Ager.* Chicago: Thomas More Press, 1982.

Programs:

Dinkmeyer, Don and McKay, Gary D. *Systematic Training for Effective Parenting of Teens.* Circle Pines, MN: American Guidance Service, 1983.

An inservice program presenting a systematic and practical approach to helping parents change their approaches to working with teens. This program is designed to provide audio tapes, a Leader's Manual, and a Parent Handbook. The focus of the program includes Dreikur's Goals of Misbehavior plus three additional goals from the authors, communication skills, group skills, and lots of ideas for dealing with social and discipline situations with adolescents.

The material is an excellent follow-up and support program for your work with **You've Got To Be Kid-ding!** A Look At Adolescents.

Glenn, H. Stephen. *Developing Capable People.* Contact: American Training Center, P.O. Box 3140, Boulder, CO 80307

An inservice program for educators focusing on the development of the three perceptions and four skills necessary for people to behave in a capable manner throughout their lives. Designed as either a self-help program through the use of audiotapes and a study guide or as a group program facilitated by a leader. In the latter format, a leader's manual is included with the program. An excellent reinforcement material for the ideas presented in **You've Got To Be Kid-ding!** A Look at Adolescents.

Audiotapes:

Schuler, Robert. *Possibility Thinking.* Chicago: Nightingale-Conant, 1979.
Waitley, Denis E. *The Psychology of Winning.* Chicago: Nightingale-Conant, 1979.